EMOTIONAL REGULATION SKILLS TO OVERCOME TOXIC THINKING AND BEHAVIOR

GET OUT OF YOUR HEAD AND CALM YOUR THOUGHTS
WITH PRACTICAL STRATEGIES AND EXERCISES; STOP
ANGER, ANXIETY, JEALOUSY, AND INSECURITY

S. S. LEIGH

Special Bonus!

Want This Bonus Book for FREE?

Get <u>FREE</u>, unlimited access to it and all my new books by joining the Fan Base!

SCAN W/ YOUR CAMERA TO JOIN!

CONTENTS

Introduction   11

1. UNDERSTANDING HOW EMOTIONS,
   THOUGHTS, AND BEHAVIOR ARE
   INTERCONNECTED   17
   Unconventional but Tried and Tested
   Techniques   22
   Thoughts Occur in Loops and Stem from
   Beliefs   23
   Exercise   26
   Evaluate Your Thoughts   27
   Emotions and Behavior Occur in Patterns   32
   Exercise   33

2. THE ROLE OF TRAUMAS AND BELIEFS   39
   Exercise   46
   Beliefs Shape Our Reality   51
   Exercise   55

3. EVALUATE, DESIGN, AND OPTIMIZE YOUR
   EXTERNAL ENVIRONMENT   61
   Exercise   66
   The Role of Your Physical Environment   69
   Exercise   75

4. MASTERING YOUR INNER WORLD   81
   Give up Judgment   83
   Exercise   86
   Your Thoughts Reveal a Lot About Your Inner
   and Outer World   90
   Exercise   97

5. YOUR EXTERNAL SUPPORT SYSTEM   99
   Getting to the Root of Things   101
   Exercise   104

Your External Support System   108
Express Your Needs Using "I" Statements   109
Be Willing to Have Difficult Conversations   112
Exercise   114
Seek Out Others Who Can Help You   115
Exercise   116

6. UNDERSTANDING NEEDS AND
BOUNDARIES   117
What Does it Mean to Have Strong
Boundaries?   119
Exercise   123
Understanding Your Responses to the Exercise
Above   127
Stop Over-giving   130
Exercise   132
How to be a Good Receiver   134
Exercise   135

7. HANDLING INTENSE EMOTIONS AND
EMOTIONAL BREAKDOWNS   137
What Are Intense Emotions?   138
What is an Emotional Breakdown?   139
The Difference Between Experiencing Intense
Emotions and Having an Emotional
Breakdown   140
The Call-it-Out Aloud Technique   142
Venting Through Writing   144
Deep Breathing   145
Move Your Body   146
Positive Self-Talk   147
How to Deal with an Emotional Breakdown   150
Focus on Maintaining a Routine   151
Invest in Self-Care   151
Spend Time with Trusted Loved Ones   152
Join Support Groups   152

8. PRACTICING MINDFULNESS,
MEDITATION, AND GUIDED JOURNALING
EXERCISES   155
Practicing Mindfulness   158
The Practice   159
Mindfulness on the Go   161
Stress Release Meditation   163
The Practice   164
Guided Journaling Exercises   167
The Practice   168

Conclusion   173
References   177

Learn to use your emotions to think, not think with your emotions.

— ROBERT KIYOSAKI

INTRODUCTION

Emotions are a beautiful thing – they enable us to experience life in all its richness and fullness. Untamed emotions, on the other hand, can cause us enormous distress and suffering. Learning to regulate one's emotions is hands-down the single most important skill one must master in order to live a truly fulfilling life.

From my own experience, I have come to believe that 90% of success in any area of life boils down to one's mindset and ability to control one's emotions. Whether it is business or personal relationships, without emotional control you are likely to keep taking poor decisions that prevent you from getting what you want.

That being said, if you feel your negative emotions are spiraling out of control and you just can't stop thinking obsessively about everything that's not good for you, let me give you an assurance. You are not alone! What you are facing is a very human struggle. No one is born with emotional regulation skills. Of course, it is true that different people have innately different levels of sensitivity. But even then, emotional regulation is a skill one has to master through deliberate and intentional practice.

At this point in my life, everyone thinks that I have always been as calm and composed as I am now. Honestly, I can't help but chuckle. I wish they had seen me when I used to be a nervous wreck struggling to function properly at home and at work. My mind used to be constantly preoccupied with everything that could go wrong. Thanks to such negative thinking, I would be jittery with fear and nervousness 24/7.

Negative thoughts and negative emotions are strongly interlinked. Trying to determine which one comes first is akin to attempting to solve the classic chicken and egg conundrum. Thoughts and emotions go hand-in-hand. Negative thinking causes a surge of negative emotions and vice versa. This eventually leads to detrimental behavior patterns which prevent one from achieving one's goals and living the kind of life one desires to live.

To change detrimental behavior patterns, you have to work on transforming your thoughts and emotions. The good news is that when you work on transforming your thought patterns, your emotional state also undergoes a change.

Similarly, your emotions undergo a transformation when you become in charge of your emotions. Working on either one of these pays off enormously. In this book, I'm going to show you how to transform both your thoughts and emotions although the focus would be more on working with emotions.

This is because, from my own experience, I can tell you that working on our emotions pays off a lot more heavily than adopting a thought-centric approach. We like to think of ourselves as creatures of logic but, in reality, we are creatures of emotions. As human beings, it is easier for us to suspend logic than to suspend our emotions. There is plenty of research that shows how most of our life is run by our emotions. That isn't a bad thing in itself. The question is what kind of emotions are running our life.

Emotions can give us a powerful motivation to accomplish seemingly impossible feats – something that logic alone can never do to us. For instance, just imagine what a mother would do to save her baby who is trapped inside a burning house. You need that kind of fire and drive to achieve big things in life. It is impossible to foster it through logic alone. Logic is helpful for making sound decisions but you need passion and emotional intensity to achieve great things.

Having negative emotions like anger, fear, or anxiety isn't necessarily a bad thing. It is what you do with them that determines whether these emotions are serving you or acting against you. You can use all your negative emotions for positive action. With the right attitude, negative emotions can serve as the rocket fuel that launches you to achieve your goals.

As human beings, we must experience the full spectrum of emotions. No emotion is to be denied, suppressed, or avoided. In fact, what we resist persists. The goal is to accept, embrace, and experience all your emotions without being negatively impacted by them. If you have no idea right now how that is even possible, don't worry. I am here for you. I'll show you how you can do it.

Mastering and regulating your emotions doesn't imply you'll never experience any negative emotions. A lot of coaches teach this approach but it's not healthy at all. Denying, suppressing, or resisting emotions is akin to stuffing all your clutter into a closet. You close the doors and think all the clutter has been removed from your space. It only lasts until the day the doors of the closet burst open and the clutter spreads everywhere once again. Our emotions work in exactly the same way. Emotional suppression causes a person to blow up at the most unexpected times and inopportune moments.

In this book, I'll show you how you can master your emotions without suppressing, denying, or resisting them. There is no such thing as a quick fix. Emotional mastery requires time, effort, and practice. But the good news is that even a little effort pays huge dividends. Emotional regulation is the most important skill you are ever going to have in your arsenal. Life is a lot simpler and easier when you have control over your emotions.

Emotional regulation is a skill that anyone can develop and master. It doesn't matter what your past has been like. You can acquire emotional mastery even if you have been told your whole life you are "too emotional" for your own good. Everything can be changed. Becoming the person you have always wanted to be is entirely in your own hands. If I can do it, then so can you! As I shared with you earlier, there was a time in my life when I had no control over my emotions. Now, I live life with calmness, composure, and tremendous self-control.

In this book, I have strived to share with you everything I have learned along the way to become the person that I am today. If you'd follow what I am sharing, then you'll get the same results. That's just inevitable!

.

1

UNDERSTANDING HOW EMOTIONS, THOUGHTS, AND BEHAVIOR ARE INTERCONNECTED

"Thoughts create emotions, emotions create feelings and feelings create behavior. So it's very important that our thoughts are positive, to attract the right people, events and circumstances into our lives."

— AVIS WILLIAMS

To understand how emotions, thoughts, and behavior are interconnected, we have to first define each one. So let us start with the first one – what is an emotion? I think this definition sums it up quite well: "An emotion occurs when there are certain biological, certain experiential, and certain cognitive states which all occur simultaneously." (Mayer, n.d.)

It is safe to assume that emotions are an essential part of the feedback mechanism of the human psyche. Emotions help guide our actions or at times misguide our actions (when we allow our emotions to control us instead of exercising control over it).

Now, let us look at the definition of thought: "The terms thought and thinking refer to conscious cognitive processes that can happen independently of sensory stimulation." (Wikipedia, n.d.) In other words, thoughts arise of their own accord. That being said, the experience of certain emotions can also lead to specific thoughts.

Thoughts and emotions often lead to behavior. "Behavior is how someone acts. It is what a person does to make something happen, to make something change, or to keep things the same. Behavior is a response to things that are happening: internally - thoughts and feelings; externally - the environment, including other people." (NSW Health, n.d.)

Since these three are powerfully interlinked, any change to either of the three would lead to an automatic influence on the other two. Hence, if we are struggling with negative thoughts or negative emotions, an intentional positive change in behavior will impact our thoughts and emotions as well. In practice, what does this look like?

So let us say you have been feeling overwhelmed by negative thoughts and emotions. You recognize what is going on. In order to change your state, you intentionally schedule an activity that you enjoy. For instance, having a fun day at an amusement park or maybe just going for a walk in your favorite park. Performing an enjoyable activity will automatically have a powerful influence on your mind and your emotions.

Personally, this is my favorite way of changing my state. The effect is almost immediate. Moving your body compels your emotions and thoughts to also shift. If you'll remain stuck at a place while negative thoughts and emotions overwhelm you, it will be very hard to disperse such a state by using mental and emotional strategies alone. Of course, they have their own place and I am not undermining their importance in any way. I feel it is best to combine different strategies together to transform your state.

That being said, you can also impact your behavior by working only on your thoughts or on your emotions. Of course, it will require more effort as getting your mind to think a certain way or your emotions to be channelized in a certain direction is much harder than simply jumping into action. In my experience, techniques for transforming thoughts and emotions work best in conjunction to behavioral modifications. If you do all three, success is guaranteed!

For now, let us say you wanted to work on your thoughts. You can use affirmations to transform your negative thinking. I often advise my clients to write down their negative thoughts on a sheet of paper and then write statements that are exactly the opposite of what they initially wrote down on another sheet of paper. These new positive statements are their affirmations. I suggest tearing down and burning the first sheet and then frequently repeating the new positive affirmations they created.

Affirmations become powerful when they are repeated often. If you can get yourself to feel what you are saying as if it were already true, you will get results very fast. Ideally, affirmations should always be repeated with emotions. However, when you are starting out, it may be hard to get yourself to feel all the emotions. You can use visualization to feel what the words convey. But be patient.

Over time, you will definitely start feeling the truth encapsulated in the words you are repeating. As you can see, transforming your state by using affirmations may take longer than using a positive activity to do the same. Ideally, you want to combine both because you need long-term transformation by changing your thought processes and emotional patterns. In the short term, getting your body moving and engaging in productive activities often turns out to be the most effective strategy. Combined with tools for transforming thought patterns and emotions, it becomes even more effective.

So now, if we were working only on emotions what would it look like? To transform the emotional state, I often advise my clients to use the power of memory. The mind can't tell the difference between what is imagined and what is real. When you are watching a horror movie, your body undergoes the same physiological reactions as what would occur if you were facing a threatening situation in real life. You can use this knowledge to your advantage by intentionally imagining a pleasant scenario or even watching a movie that evokes positive emotions in you.

There are three ways in which you can do this:

- Recall a time in your past when you felt safe, supported, and happy. Go back to that moment in time and relive all the emotions you felt there.
- Think of a scene from a movie or TV show that evokes a strong positive emotional response in you. Watch this scene repeatedly allowing yourself to fully experience the emotions that arise through the experience.
- Create a vision of a personal heaven. Close your eyes and visualize your ideal world where you feel loved, supported, and cared for. Allow yourself to feel all the positive emotions that arise.

Of course, doing these exercises requires more effort as you have to intentionally shift your focus from what is causing you anxiety to what would soothe you. As I said earlier, ideally, you want to combine different techniques to work on your thoughts, emotions, and behavior simultaneously. But I also want you to test out working on each of these aspects individually so you'll see for yourself how working on any one aspect immediately impacts the other two.

If you haven't tested out the techniques I shared with you, go back and re-read this section and test out all the different ideas I presented here. Yes, you can do it even if you are in a pleasant state mentally and emotionally. In fact, that is even better as you'll be able to observe more clearly how strongly these three aspects are interlinked.

If you are distressed in any way, then these techniques will definitely help you self-soothe. Go ahead and give them a try if you haven't tested them out yet. Come back to the rest of the chapter once you are done. Reading a book won't change your life but putting into practice what I am teaching you here will definitely have a massive positive impact on your life.

UNCONVENTIONAL BUT TRIED AND TESTED TECHNIQUES

A lot of my techniques may seem somewhat unconventional and different from what you would find professionals practicing. I am sharing these techniques with you because I have successfully used them to heal my own trauma. I use these methods and techniques to manage my emotions to this day. I won't share anything with you that I haven't tested out myself and that hasn't worked for me personally or for my clients.

Life is all about trial and error. To keep growing and evolving into the highest version of yourself, you have to test out different things. Some may work for you and some may not. Pick the ones that work for you and adopt them into your daily life. Always remember that you are the only one who knows what works best for you.

After using each technique, ask yourself, "How am I feeling?" Check to see if there has been any positive effect for you. You don't need to intellectually understand everything. In fact, trying to intellectualize everything can easily turn into a trap that never allows you to make any real progress. Instead, focus on and trust your own experience. Experiential learning is the best type of learning – only what you experience for yourself can be truly real for you.

THOUGHTS OCCUR IN LOOPS AND STEM FROM BELIEFS

When you are feeling overwhelmed by thoughts, it seems like there are too many of them to deal with. If instead of allowing them to loosely flow around in your mind, you'd take the time to sit down and write them, you'll discover something different. You'll realize that there aren't really that many thoughts plaguing and overwhelming you. Instead, it is some thoughts that get repeated over and over again.

Most likely, what you were thinking yesterday is what you are thinking today. What you are thinking today is what you'll be thinking tomorrow and so on. To change your thoughts, you have to intentionally choose differently. Since thoughts occur in loops, working on some thoughts that appear repeatedly will completely transform your thinking experience.

I am sure you have heard the saying that the mind is a wonderful servant but a terrible master. If you'll allow your untamed thoughts to run your life and guide your actions, you'll never achieve anything worthwhile. An untamed mind is like a garden that hasn't been tended to. You can't expect to experience beauty in such a garden. Weeds grow there and unpleasantness resides there. Your mind is your private garden. It depends entirely upon you to tend to it like a beautiful garden or leave it untended to.

You must also realize that your thoughts are your perceptions – they are your ideas of how things are or how they may be. They are not always rooted in reality. The vast majority of our thoughts stem from our belief system – what we believe to be true about the world, about ourselves, about our future, etc.

To transform your thoughts, you have to also work on your beliefs. The problem is that most people never sit down to question their beliefs – they take them for granted as if they were an objective reality true for everyone. What you believe in is what you think about. What you think about is what you experience in your reality.

Most of your beliefs are not even your own. They have been given to you by society, parents, teachers, and other people who played an influential role when you were growing up. These beliefs are reflections of what other people believed to be true for themselves and not what is actually true for you. For instance, maybe you were told, "You are so bad at math." At some point, you started believing in this statement. Once you start believing that something is impossible to achieve, you'll never put in the effort to improve yourself in that area.

If you believe you are bad at math, then espousing that belief immediately implies you'll consciously and subconsciously reject all possibilities of improving yourself at it. You are bad at math is someone else's idea that you accepted as your own belief. No matter what anyone else says, math is a skill that can be learned. You can teach yourself to be good at it but for that, you'll have to drop your limiting belief. You'll have to intentionally relinquish the idea that you are bad at math.

To transform your belief at the core level, you'll have to prop up a new belief by espousing new thoughts. This could mean repeating affirmations throughout the day and using positive self-talk. For our example, the affirmation can be, "I am brilliant at math!" Whenever you start feeling doubts and fears creep up, use positive self-talk like, "I know I can do this!" "I have the ability and the power to do this." "I am committed – getting better and improving every day is my only choice!"

EXERCISE

Write down all the thoughts that are on your mind right now. I would highly recommend writing with a pen in a journal. Typing is also okay. It's just that I have found writing with an actual pen on a physical paper compels us to be more present with our thoughts. You can do either but I would recommend physically writing things down if that's possible for you.

For the next three days, I want you to carry this journal with you everywhere you go. Whenever you start feeling overwhelmed, write down your thoughts. The simple act of writing everything down will help you feel lighter and less overwhelmed.

The process of writing also helps you distance yourself from your thoughts. Always remember that you are not your thoughts. Your thoughts are a part of you but they are not you. You don't have to judge yourself over the undesirable thoughts you get. Let them rise and fall like waves in an ocean.

Writing your thoughts down helps you look at them more objectively. You gain a different perspective when you read what you have written down. Also, the process of writing disperses a lot of the emotional charge that are associated with those thoughts. Journaling is, therefore, an excellent tool for managing and releasing difficult emotions.

By reading and evaluating what you have written down, you gain a fresh perspective. This helps you understand the direction in which you and your life are going. When you understand that, then you can direct the sails of your thoughts, emotions, and actions in your desired direction.

EVALUATE YOUR THOUGHTS

At the end of the three day period, it is time to process and evaluate your thoughts.

Read through everything and answer the following questions.

What are the recurring themes – thought patterns that are being repeated over and over again. For example; worries about finances, fear of marriage breaking down, etc. Try to identify the theme behind the frequently recurring thought patterns.

What is the one recurring theme that is bothering you the most right now? Pick the one that is weighing on you the heaviest resolving which will give you the greatest relief for now.

_____

_____

_____

_____

What are the negative thoughts associated with this theme? For instance, if you theme is financial worries, your thoughts can be something like this: I am never going to make enough money, I am afraid of losing money, etc.

_____

_____

_____

_____

_____

_____

_____

_____

What evidence do you have to support the legitimacy of these negative thoughts? Next to each negative thought write down the evidence you have to support its legitimacy. If there is no evidence or reason why you should believe that thought, then write down "no evidence." Feel free to use another sheet of paper if you run out of space here.

Evaluate the list you created. How many of your thoughts are legitimate in the sense that there is concrete evidence that you should believe these negative thoughts as truths? I am sure very few of those thoughts can be justified. Negative thoughts rooted in fear and anxiety arise from the limbic system which is associated with the fight or flight response.

We can't think rationally when fear takes over as even the smallest of threats is perceived as a life-or-death situation.

The good news is that you can train yourself to calm down and see the negative thoughts for what they really are – mostly irrational fears and illogical anxiety-inducing ideas. Note down the total number of thoughts that are completely irrational as in there is no evidence or legitimate reason why you should believe them as truths.

Now, go back and evaluate those thoughts that are justified in some way. For instance, maybe there is a 50% chance what you are afraid of can turn out to be true. Let me give you an example. Let us say your friend hasn't phoned you in a month. You fear they have severed all contact with you. There is a 50% chance that this can be true. But isn't there a 50% chance that they just got busy and life took over. Maybe they just haven't had a chance to get back to you because of how intense things got in their own life.

What is much healthier and better for you to believe? Choose the thoughts that are best for you and that serve your highest good. Another thing I'll tell you here is something I learned from a mentor of mine. He taught me an important lesson, "Never believe anything as the truth until you have concrete evidence to support its veracity." If you don't have concrete evidence to support your fear that your friend is intentionally ignoring you, then isn't it better to believe that they just got busy or have something going on in their own life which has nothing to do with you?

Write down those thoughts that are justified in some way, and then assess what is best for you to believe in.

EMOTIONS AND BEHAVIOR OCCUR IN PATTERNS

Just like how thoughts occur in loops, emotions and behavior occur in patterns. Think of that time when you thought, "Why do I keep doing this? I don't understand why I can't stop?" We do certain things because they have become established patterns for us. The same goes for emotions. We feel the same kind of emotions frequently and repeatedly because they have become part of our emotional patterns.

This is also the reason why so many people jump from one relationship to another. The face and name may change but the relationship they have with the other person remains the same. They find themselves acting in the same way feeling the same kind of emotions that they felt in the previous relationship. This is because we are constantly attracting people, situations, and circumstances that are aligned with our beliefs about the world.

You may think that the other person is the problem but if you keep experiencing the same thing over and over with different people, then you have to look at the common denominator in all those connections – you! I know how hard this is but you have to step into your power by taking 100% responsibility for your life. Taking responsibility doesn't mean condoning other people's bad behavior and feeling guilty or blaming yourself.

On the contrary, taking responsibility is all about claiming your power in every situation. You don't have control over how other people act but you have full control over your own actions. When you focus on what you can control in any situation, you feel powerful. When you blame others, you give your power away. This is not about who is right or who is wrong. It is about choosing what helps you feel powerful and moves you closer to your goals.

Your feelings, emotions, and thoughts influence your actions. For instance, if you aren't feeling confident and good about yourself, you'll act in ways that will confirm your negative beliefs about yourself. On the other hand, if you can get yourself to feel confident and content with who you are, you'll act in ways that will confirm your positive beliefs about yourself.

As I said earlier, thoughts, emotions, and behavior are strongly interlinked. You can influence your behavior by transforming how you feel about yourself but you can also influence how you feel about yourself by intentionally changing your actions. For instance, you can do things that will help your self-confidence. Whenever you start feeling bad about yourself, you can reference those times when you achieved something significant that boosted your confidence, it will help you in the present as well.

EXERCISE

For the next three days, carry a journal with you. Note down your thoughts at regular intervals but this time focus more on how you are feeling. Do this exercise every couple of hours – like at regular intervals of 2-3 hours. Do it when you are feeling good, when you are feeling neutral, when you are feeling negative, and everything in between. You want to accumulate enough data to analyze your emotional state.

Every time you create an entry focus on asking the following questions:

- What am I feeling right now?
- Where exactly in my body am I feeling these emotions?
- What is the behavior that these emotions are prompting you to engage in?

At the end of the three-day period, analyze the data you have collected and record your answers to the following questions.

What are the predominant emotions that you feel throughout the day? Like, anger, hatred, happiness, joy, etc.

Which one emotion do you experience most often? How does it make you feel? Like, if it is anger does it make you bitter, resentful, judgmental, critical, etc.?

Where exactly in your body do you feel this emotion?

What kind of action/s does this emotion prompt you to take?

Do you like the action/s you have been taking or are feeling tempted to take? Write down your reason explaining why you like or don't like the action/s you feel compelled to take.

If you don't like the action/s you have been taking, what can you do to change? For instance, perhaps you can spend some time with this emotion and decide to not do anything in the heat of the moment. Give yourself a few hours to allow your emotional state to calm down before taking any action.

By completing these exercises you'll realize just how strongly linked your thoughts, emotions, and behavior are. Always remember that self-awareness is the master key to trans-formation.

Be sure to complete all these exercises before moving on to the next chapter where we will discuss the two main coping strategies that everyone uses for processing their thoughts and emotions.

2

THE ROLE OF TRAUMAS AND BELIEFS

"Your beliefs... your thoughts... your emotions... shape your life. Like magnets, they function to manifest occurrences in a chosen reality. What you most believe comes into your Life."

— ELLE NICOLAI

I f you find yourself obsessively thinking about everything that can possibly go wrong and/or you often suffer from negative moods, the answer lies in your childhood. The blueprint for how we are going to experience life gets established pretty early on in childhood. To improve our adult relationships, whether with others or with our own self, we have to go back to the first relationship we formed with our primary caregivers.

I realized this fact a long time ago. For years, I struggled with dysfunctional relationships. I'll meet someone wonderful. Things would start out on a high note. The other person will be extremely invested in me. I would become convinced I have finally met the person I have been waiting for my whole life. Just when things would become extremely intense, the other person would back out a little. From that point on, things would get progressively worse. The harder I would try to salvage the relationship, the faster it would disintegrate.

I thought I was doomed or maybe cursed. It made no sense why I kept experiencing the same relationship pattern over and over again with different people. I started wondering if there was something wrong with me that made me undesirable when someone got too close to me. I also wondered if it was destiny to remain single and because of that none of the relationships ever worked out.

One day while casually browsing the psychology section of my favorite bookstore, I stumbled upon a book on attachment theory which was formulated by a psychiatrist called John Bowlby (Wikipedia, n.d.). I opened the book and read a few pages. What I read left my mouth agape – I had read a description of my own relationship pattern described with painful accuracy within the pages of the book. The more I learned about attachment theory, the clearer it became to me why my adult relationships were dysfunctional. It didn't have much to do with the present but had everything to do with my extremely challenging childhood.

I was the fourth child of my parents. Apparently, I was "a mistake" – I spent my entire childhood feeling like I didn't matter. My parents were very poor – they struggled to make ends meet. There was constant fighting and bickering over money. I am not entirely sure why they married each other because there was certainly no love in their relationship. My father was also openly cheating on my mother. My mother lacked the courage to walk out of the relationship. Even though she was making a living of her own, she felt psychologically and emotionally dependent upon her marriage.

Due to her own struggles and challenges, my mother was often in a bad mood. I felt unwanted and invisible. If I ever asked for something, she would blow up and make me feel guilty that I asked for anything at all. The idea that I was all alone became deeply embedded in my mind. I decided that if I ever wanted anything, I'd have to figure out how to get it on my own. I was just not one of those lucky children whose parents look after their every need. I felt deeply and profoundly alone in this world.

Even though I was the youngest child, I often took care of my older siblings. I would compromise with my own needs to cater to the needs of others because deep within, I felt that my own needs don't matter. As I described earlier, my mother had an explosive temper. I was scared of her unpredictable moods. She would blow up anytime, anywhere without even the slightest provocation.

The environment at home was so depressing that my heart used to sink at the idea of returning back home after school. For me, home was a place of pain, misery, dissatisfaction, disappointment, and dysfunction. I often dreamed of a happy family life. I would think to myself – one day I'll get married have my own family and every day of my life would be joyful.

Later on, as I studied attachment theory and learned about the damages that emotionally immature parents cause to their children, I realized that my dream of a happy family life was actually a "healing fantasy." Having the fantasy of a perfect life helped me cope with all the chaos and unhappiness that characterized my home life.

Later on, as I got older and started dating, I was very quick to fall in love and get attached. Only after I learned more about attachment styles and the concept of a healing fantasy that I realized all my life I had been looking for someone to give me the childhood I never had. I was so desperate to have the happy idyllic family life that I ignored all the red flags when I picked people who were damaged and wounded.

Indeed, not working through and healing our wounds make us vulnerable to forming relationships with other damaged and wounded people. In our society, instant chemistry – the type that sends chills down your spine and makes you obsessed with another person – is often glorified. Many people get married believing that life with their lover would be like a gondola ride through the glorious canals of Venice. Instead, a little while later, they realize the other person is just as imperfect as everyone else. Being with someone does require work. It also requires radical unconditional acceptance of oneself and one's partner.

When old wounds come to the surface to be healed in intimate relationships, people think they have fallen out of love with the other person. They don't want to do the work of looking within and healing the wounds that have been triggered and brought to the surface by the presence of their partner. Instead, they erroneously place the blame for their pain on their partner and hop from one relationship to another searching for that one perfect person who will "save" them.

I was waiting to be saved and every time someone showed me the possibility of having a happy family life and then disappeared from my life, I felt depressed and dejected. Once I started understanding my attachment style, it became clear to me that my experiences in the present were rooted in the past. I had to go back to my childhood and start healing my extreme fear of abandonment. I had felt abandoned by my family – I was waiting to be saved by someone who could give me the childhood I never had.

Due to my extreme fear of abandonment, I was perpetually in a hyper-vigilant stage – looking for signs that the other person is going to leave me. I'd remain at the edge of my seat waiting for the last show to drop. It became a self-fulfilling prophecy. Through my intimate relationships, I was getting to relive and re-experience the feeling of being abandoned that had characterized my early childhood experiences.

Interestingly enough, I was constantly attracting and being attracted to partners who were anxious avoidant – individuals who had also been damaged in their childhood. Instead of becoming anxious preoccupied, they became anxious avoidant. The former makes a person obsessed with seeking intimacy with other people while the latter revolve around a deep fear of experiencing authentic intimacy with another person.

I am sharing this story with you to help you understand how our beliefs, thoughts, and behavior patterns get shaped by our early childhood experiences. Most of the things we believe to be true are not our own beliefs but what we picked up from the belief system of our primary caregivers. The thoughts we think frequently stem from our belief system. We can transform our behavior patterns in the present only by healing our childhood traumas. We must go back in time and transform the beliefs, ideas, and thoughts we picked up from our primary caregivers that don't serve our highest good.

The good news is that we are highly programmable beings. The ignorance of our caregivers programmed us in the wrong way. I am not suggesting that we should be angry or bitter toward them. Keep in mind, they did the best that they were capable of based on the knowledge and understanding they had. It is likely that their caregivers didn't treat them any better so how they treated us was just a result of what they had learned from those who came before them.

No matter what you have experienced, blaming others should not be an option. Not because you should condone other people's wrong actions but because the moment you put the blame on someone else, you give the power away. If someone else is responsible for how you are feeling and living your life, you hand over your power to them. Instead, you can take 100% responsibility for who you are and how you feel. By doing this, you instantly become more powerful. When you ask yourself what you can do now to create the life you want and to be the highest version of yourself, you reclaim your power.

Once I realized that my early childhood had given me an anxious preoccupied attachment style, I was able to ask myself the question, "How can I heal myself and turn this negative into a positive?" Indeed, life is all about turning our weaknesses into strengths. Your greatest challenges are your greatest opportunities for growth. My early childhood experience didn't automatically provide me with a secure attachment style that could support healthy adult relationships but it was in my hands to develop a secure attached style. I learned self-soothing techniques and methods to calm myself when bouts of anxiety would engulf me. Don't worry,

I'll share some of the best techniques with you in this book as well. Learning to self-soothe is absolutely essential for emotional regulation.

Over time, with tremendous self-awareness and an unwavering commitment to healing my inner child, I developed a secure attachment style. There are days when bouts of anxiety become to resurface but now, I have the knowledge to manage it appropriately. I have been married for a long time now to a partner who also has a secure attachment style. In life, at any point of time, you can become whoever you want to be.

Turning your life around is entirely in your own hands. The question is are you fully committed to changing your life? If the answer is yes, then continue reading on. You are on your way to an incredibly exciting and rewarding life. If the answer is no, then, sit back and take your time to reflect – what is it that's holding you back from taking full responsibility and committing to turn all your dreams into reality?

EXERCISE

Take a few moments to close your eyes and think about a traumatic experience from your childhood. Some people become triggered by the mere suggestion that there can be traumatic experiences in their childhood. Pretty much everyone in this world has suffered some kind of trauma or another. If you are struggling to recall such an experience, then just relax by breathing deeply. Let your mind take you to whatever negative experience comes up first irrespective of the age you were at.

It is going to be hard but allow yourself to fully relive that experience. Write down your thought and feelings about that experience in as much detail as possible. If you run out of space here, then use a separate sheet to continue writing down your thoughts and feelings. Write for as long as you need to. After pouring everything down on paper, you'll feel lighter, especially if you have never shared the details about this incident with anyone yet.

How has this incident impacted your life? What changed in you and your life after this incident?

Do you like who you have become because of this incident? I would urge you to not think of things as black and white. The beauty of life lies in its complexity. There are many shades of grey. While the incident may have had a negative impact on you, there is also a chance that it has contributed to your growth and evolution. If the latter isn't true yet, then that is how you can use this incident to create a better life for yourself and become a more evolved version of yourself.

Write an apology letter to your younger self expressing how sorry you are that you allowed your inner child to suffer so much (Your inner child lives inside you no matter how many candles you have had on your birthday cake). Tell your inner child that you are deeply sorry that you couldn't take a stand for yourself at that time but from now on, you'll always be there for yourself.

You are the only one who can save you. You must begin now by fully committing to standing by your own side no matter what. Whatever it is that you didn't receive from others, you have the power to give to yourself. You just need to decide that you are ready and willing to do whatever it takes to always be there for yourself.

In the letter, be sure to express all the love and care that you wish you had received from someone else at the time. Give it to yourself like you were your own best friend looking after yourself. You can use the space here to write the letter. If you run out of space, then feel free to use separate sheets to continue writing.

BELIEFS SHAPE OUR REALITY

Beliefs are the blueprint that shape our experience of reality. If you don't like anything in your reality, you can't change it by fighting the manifestation you are seeing in the outer world. Instead, you'll have to go inside and explore the beliefs that have birthed those experiences in the outer world. Think of it like this – if you were watching a movie in a movie theatre, you won't fight the projections on the screen. Instead, you'll change the reel that is being played.

To change the reel that is getting projected on the screen of your life, you'll have to work on your beliefs. I am not talking about what you believe to be true at the conscious level. Your conscious thoughts and ideas don't impact your reality to the extent that your subconscious beliefs do. Your beliefs are thoughts and ideas that you have accepted as truths. Many of them serve you and many don't. You have to identify the ones that are holding you back and replace them with new empowering beliefs that serve your highest good.

"This is how humans are: We question all our beliefs, except for the ones that we really believe in, and those we never think to question."

— ORSON SCOTT CARD

As this quote suggests pausing to question our deeply held beliefs is one of the hardest things in the world. We often mistake negative beliefs for facts. I'll share another story with you that will illustrate how this works.

When I was in second grade, I joined a singing class. One day our teacher asked each one of us to sign a few lines individually. When my turn came, I did my best but to my horror, everyone except the teacher laughed at me. I felt so embarrassed that I wished I could just disappear into the earth at that moment. The kids mocked me for being an awful singer. Interestingly enough, till that point, I had never thought I was a bad singer. But because of what I was told, I accepted the idea that I was an awful singer as a fact.

I never made any effort to improve my singing skills. After all, what was the point when I already knew I was an awful singer? I created this reality for myself where there was no possibility for ever becoming a better singer. The belief that I was a bad singer was handed over to me by society and I accepted it as my reality.

Many years passed and I never again dared to sing publicly. A few years back I became friends with someone who is a classical singer. She would often remark to me, "You have such a wonderful voice, you should try singing." I wasn't sure why she would think I had a voice fit for singing when could barely sing a line without subjecting myself to embarrassment and ridicule.

One day I agreed to accompany her to a singing workshop she was conducting for aspiring singers. I was really nervous to sing again publicly but this time, no one laughed at me. Instead, I received encouragement. I was told I have a good voice, and I just need to work on my rhythm and pitch. This feedback got me excited. I wanted to see if I could become good at something I had believed my entire life I was bad at.

I started learning the right techniques for singing. I practiced regularly. I am proud to say that at this stage of my life most people in my life think that I am an amazing singer. Teaching myself to sing was an exercise in breaking a belief system that was holding me back from realizing my full potential in life. I accepted someone else's opinion of me as a fact for what I can do and who I can be in this life. It was also an opportunity for me to heal the trauma of being mocked and shamed.

I may not have had inborn musical talent but that doesn't mean I was doomed to be a terrible singer my entire life. There are many things we can teach ourselves by sheer determination and force of will.

In the book Mindset, Carol Dweck explains the difference between a fixed mindset and a growth mindset. What we believe to be true about our talents and abilities has the strongest impact on our success or lack of it. People with a fixed mindset believe that we either have certain abilities or we don't. Those who have a growth mindset believe that abilities can be developed. It may not be easy but it is definitely possible! One of my favorite quotes from the book is, "It's not always the people who start out the smartest who end up the smartest." (Dweck, 2007)

I really want you to sit down and think about who you want to be in this life and how you want to live your life. This book is about regulating emotions but our emotions and thoughts don't occur in isolation. They are connected to who we are, what we believe to be true, and the goals that we set for ourselves. Most people drift through life without ever deciding clearly who they want to be and how they want to live their life.

When you know what kind of person you want to be, you'll also know what kind of thoughts and emotions would be associated with that person. Similarly, the ideal life you want to live would be supported by certain thoughts, emotions, and beliefs. Without a goal, you'll never be able to give a clear direction to your mind and heart.

Once you have identified your goals, you'll need to look at the thoughts, ideas, and beliefs that are holding you back from living your dream life. You'll have to transform them into thoughts, ideas, and beliefs that support you. The exercises I am going to share with you now will help you in this process. Be sure to complete all the exercises before moving on to the next chapter. Always remember that your life is not going to change by reading a book. It is going to change only when you are doing the work to transform your life.

EXERCISE

Write a description of your ideal self – don't hold yourself back. Think of it like making a Christmas wish. What would you write if I told you that whatever you are writing here will definitely come true? Trust me, it will! Everything is possible in this life.

What kind of thoughts, beliefs, emotions, and ideas does this person have?

Write a description of your ideal life – how you want to live, what your daily life is like, how you spend your time, etc. Again, don't hold yourself back. Think of it like making a Christmas wish. What would you write if I told you that whatever you are writing here will definitely come true? Trust me, it will! Everything is possible in this life.

What do you believe to be true right now that is preventing you from being your ideal self and living your ideal life? Is it really a belief or is it a fact? Next to each point, write down "B" for belief and "F" for a fact. For instance, you have two legs and two hands is a fact but you are terrible at math is a belief. The latter can be improved if you become committed to becoming great at math.

Most of the things we believe to be facts are actually strongly held beliefs. It is very hard to identify these beliefs. You just have to become skeptical about absolutely everything you have believed to be true so far. Some things may be a fact but even they can be changed. Like, you have brown hair may be a fact but if you don't like brown hair on yourself, then you can change it to another color you like better. Life provides us with infinite possibilities.

What practical actions can you take to turn your negative beliefs into facts? Pick one belief transforming which will have the greatest positive impact on your life right now, and then start working on it. For instance, going back to being bad at math example, you can commit to taking classes and practicing math problems daily. If you'll stick with anything long enough while doing your best to improve yourself by a marginal percentage every day constantly, a day will come when you'll become exceptional at it.

3

EVALUATE, DESIGN, AND OPTIMIZE YOUR EXTERNAL ENVIRONMENT

"You can't make positive choices for the rest of your life without an environment that makes those choices easy, natural, and enjoyable."

— DEEPAK CHOPRA

The influence of one's immediate environment can never be underestimated. Indeed, you can overcome the influence of one's environment to a very large extent but it is very hard to do it consistently, constantly, and for extended periods of time. It is akin to swimming against the tide – you can do it for a while but it begins to get really exhausting after some time.

Who we are, how we process emotions, and the thoughts we think regularly are all strongly linked to our external environment. Our external environment doesn't just comprise the physical surroundings in which we spend our days but also the people with whom we spend the vast majority of our time. By simply being around other people, we subconsciously adopt their habits, ways of thinking, and even their emotional responses.

If you surround yourself with confident and happy people, then after a while you will become like them as well. If you surround yourself with depressed and dejected people, then you will soon feel depleted. If you surround yourself with cynical and angry people, then it is only a matter of time before you'll internalize those negative qualities.

Many people get triggered by this idea. They don't want to believe that others are having such a powerful influence over them. Many people also find the idea that they are being influenced by others quite wounding to the ego. No matter how you perceive it, this is a fact of life. Who you surround yourself with determines your destiny to a great extent. Therefore, it only makes sense that positive transformation should not be limited to making changes in one's inner world. It is absolutely imperative to extend those efforts to one's external environment as well.

Honestly, I used to be one of those people who thought the environment cannot affect me. At that time, everyone in my surroundings was struggling financially. They all had a lot of limiting beliefs around money. Every time I made a little progress, I would regress back to the same level as everyone else. I was tired of living paycheck to paycheck never having enough money to live the kind of life I had always wanted to live.

One day I attended a workshop where the coach asked all of us to write down the names of the people with whom we were spending the maximum amount of our time. Later on, our coach asked us to also write down the income of each person. If we didn't know the exact amount, we could write an approximate amount.

We were asked to write down the average of everyone's income and evaluate how close our own income was to the average. Shockingly enough, my income was almost exactly at the same level as the average income of my peer group. That day I learned the most important lesson of my life. Environment often trumps willpower. I was trying hard to get out of my financial struggles but the lack of positive role models in my immediate environment was preventing me from moving forward.

As human beings, we are also strongly impacted by the mindset and attitude of the people around us. At the subconscious level, we begin to mirror the people we are constantly surrounded by. Every person has a mental model that dictates their experience of life. A person's mental model is composed of a set of ideas and beliefs that dictate their experiences through life. If you are surrounded by people who have the same challenges as you, then it will be very hard for you to overcome them.

You need to expose yourself to people who have the results you want and those who have successfully overcome the challenges you are facing. It can also be beneficial to have people around you who are in the process of overcoming the challenges you are also working on. This way you can learn from their experiences as well but if you are only surrounded by people who have no interest in overcoming those challenges, then it will be very hard for you to get positive results.

Jim Rohn famously said, "You are the average of the five people you spend the most time with." (Rohn, n.d.) I can't emphasize enough how true this is! No matter how strong your willpower is, you will inevitably get influenced by the people around you. If the people you are spending all your time with have no emotional control, then you will also struggle to manage your emotions. Once I changed my company, my life transformed rapidly.

I deliberately started surrounding myself with people who were successful and wealthy. Initially, it wasn't easy so I was spending most of my time alone. I started reading books, listening to podcasts, and watching videos featuring successful people. Over time, their mindset and attitude toward life started rubbing off on me. I also realized that successful and wealthy people have a completely different mental model of the world than those who are financially struggling. As I continued on my path of self-improvement, I started meeting people who were massively successful. Eventually, as I kept making progress, my peer group transformed completely.

No matter what your goals are, you MUST surround yourself with people who have achieved what you want to achieve. If you can't get access to them in person right now, then fret not! We are living in one of the greatest eras that humanity has witnessed. You can be in the company of the most successful people in the world with just a few clicks. Read books written by these people, listen to their podcasts, watch their interviews, and capitalize on any opportunity you can find to learn from them. By simply putting yourself in their vicinity, you'll begin to make progress.

Over time, you'll start attracting such people into your life, and as you walk continue moving forward on your own journey of self-improvement. Don't underestimate the power of the company you keep. It is truly a game changer and one of the most important things you must master in life if you want to live a fulfilling life. How each person defines success can differ from individual to individual. But the idea of success modeling remains true for everyone. To become successful at anything, you need role models who have already achieved what you want to achieve. By observing them, learning from them, and modeling your own habits and actions after theirs, you can also achieve the success they have.

EXERCISE

What are your greatest struggles right now? Feel free to list them all, and then pick one to work on for now. It should be something that improving it will have the greatest positive impact on your life. For instance, let us say this was my list: poor financial situation, poor physical health, anger issues, sadness, and despondency.

Now, if I analyze this list, it is obvious to me that poor health is impacting all areas of life. Working on improving physical health will have a positive impact on all areas of life. Use this strategy to determine which area is most urgently in need of transformation right now and then start working on it. As you make progress and get results, pick one more item from the list and work on overcoming that challenge as well. Repeat this process until you have ticked off every single item of your list.

Name five people with whom you are spending the vast majority of your time. Do they have the same struggle as the one you have just committed to overcoming? Write down a "yes" or a "no" next to each person's name.

If the answer is "yes," then it would be in your best interest to figure out how you can limit your time around them. In a lot of cases, it may be difficult to not remain in physical proximity to that person. You can work on establishing strong boundaries with them. Tell them what you are willing to talk to about them and which topics you would rather avoid.

Avoid discussing your struggles with them when they have the same ones and they aren't committed to overcoming those struggles. If you can really limit the amount of time you spend with them, then that would be the best strategy. Like, you could totally disconnect or limit seeing them to a few special days a year. When you do meet them, stick to pleasant neutral topics that don't require deep conversations.

If the answer is "no," then you can use them as a positive role model and learn from them. Ask them if they have ever faced the challenge that you are facing and how they overcame it. Observe what kind of habits and attitudes they have that you can also cultivate. Try to observe them keenly and learn as much from them as possible. Focus on what they are doing differently that you can also apply to your life and then test it out.

Name five people who have the kind of results you want for yourself. Next to each person's name write down how you can bring yourself in their proximity and learn from them. Like, if it is someone you know in person, you can invite them to play golf together or capitalize on any other common interest you both have. Always seek to add value by learning what you can do for them instead of trying to use others for your own benefit.

If it is a famous person you admire, then make note of all the resources through which you can learn more about them. Like, by reading their books, listening to their interviews, etc. Pay attention to how they are living their life not only vis-à-vis the primary area of focus you have right now but in all areas of life. Of course, no one is an expert at everything.

You have to use your discretion to decide what you want to learn from someone and where it is not worth listening to them. Different people have different expertise. The secret to learning effectively from everyone is to always have your filter on. The most successful people in the world have powerful filters in place through which they sift all information to decide what's useful and what's not.

THE ROLE OF YOUR PHYSICAL ENVIRONMENT

I was struggling to complete an important project while working from home. My colleague was on the phone asking me what was going on – why was I lagging behind on the deadline? Out of sheer frustration, this colleague asked me, "Tell me, what does your environment look like right now?"

I was stunned for a few moments and then I felt ashamed. I sheepishly admitted, "It's messy." He balked and said, "That's exactly what is wrong. You can't be productive while being surrounded by so much clutter." After that, he said a line that has stayed with me my entire life, "Your physical space is a reflection of your mental space." How profound was that! Yet, until that point, I had never thought about the role that my physical environment was playing in my overall productivity and mood.

I didn't learn the lesson right away. The idea was so novel and rather strange to me that it took me a long time to truly begin to understand how strongly we are impacted by the physical environment we live in. My colleague had planted a seed in my mind. I started exploring this new idea – the correlation between one's mental environment and immediate physical space. I started observing how these two correlate for other people and not just for me.

I immediately started seeing patterns. People who were disorganized in their thoughts and lacked clarity almost always have chaotic physical environments. I also observed that every time my physical environment became too overwhelming for me that I had to begin decluttering, I felt mentally and energetically lighter. Many a time, it felt as if a heavy weight had been lifted off my shoulders.

Similarly, every time, I did some inner decluttering by mentally, emotionally, and spiritually letting go of that which wasn't serving me, I also felt a powerful urge to declutter my physical space. It is really fascinating how the inner and the outer world correlate. It is almost impossible to not have the transformation replicated in both worlds to some degree at least when one is working on either of the two aspects.

For me, this was truly a life changing revelation. I could never go back to being as messy as I used to be. Once I read Marie Kondo's *The Life-Changing Magic of Tidying Up*, it became even clearer to me that what I had learned was true and very real – our physical environment has a powerful impact upon our inner world and vice versa.

So now let me ask you this question. Put this book down for a moment and spend some time looking around. What do you see? Is your space organized, neat, and tidy? Is it messy, chaotic, and dirty? Your environment affects your moods and mental state to a much larger degree than you realize. When you are living with someone else, it becomes quite hard to have things your way but still you can try to organize and tidy your personal spaces as best as possible.

"You are a product of your environment. So choose the environment that will best develop you toward your objective. Analyze your life in terms of its environment. Are the things

around you helping you toward success - or are they holding
you back?"

— W. CLEMENT STONE

Emotional regulation has a lot to do with the physical environment we spend the vast majority of our time in. There are places that energize us and there are places that deplete us. I am sure you have experienced this before – you enter a room or a house and you suddenly start feeling drained. Even if you can't point your finger at exactly what it is, something about that environment makes you feel ill at ease. Similarly, some places have a refreshing and rejuvenating effect on us. They leave us feeling energized and vivacious.

The good news is that you can intentionally organize your environment in a way that brings you joy and peace. Colors, prints, designs, and how things are placed around a physical space all have their own unique effect on us. I would suggest that you explore and learn more about all these different aspects. I am suggesting that you need to completely redo your physical space. Such a feat may or may not be within your budget right now.

But it doesn't cost anything extra to let go of all those items that are no longer serving you and intentionally surround yourself only with those items that support the kind of life you want to live and the person that you want to be. I would highly recommend that you read Marie Kondo's *The Life-Changing Magic of Tidying Up* to learn more about decluttering.

In a lot of ways bringing order to your physical environment is the act of confronting yourself. In order to let go of things that no longer serve you or evoke any positive feelings in you, you are also getting to know yourself better. You become compelled to face things that you may not have dealt with before. Like, a gift given by an old flame may be negatively impacting your mood than adding value to your life at this point in time. Perhaps there is that tea set you inherited from your late aunt that you find really ugly but are struggling to get rid of because of its sentimental value and because you feel you'll be betraying your late aunt by giving it away. Marie addresses all these issues very tactfully in her book.

It is best to let go of items that feel more like an obligation than something you truly value and want to have around you. It is also worth exploring utilizing it for alternate purposes instead of trying to use them only for their original intended purpose. By clearing and rearranging your environment, you'll immediately make it easier for yourself to be in a pleasant mood every day. Of course, no one is ever happy 24/7 but you can optimize your environment to support positive emotions.

The act of putting your environment in order is also very useful when you are feeling ill at ease and distressed in some way. It is excellent for channelizing your energy and helping you put your energy to good use. When we are going through tough times, the natural instinct is to hide in bed and not get up at all. I am sure you have also done that at some point and it left you feeling even more dejected and drained.

In those times, having a routine really helps. I would not recommend tackling major decluttering projects during such times but stick to the routine tasks that you perform on a daily basis. Most people allow their routine to go completely haywire when things get really challenging, especially when faced with grief. During such times, sticking to a routine really helps. It provides a sense of groundedness and gives your energy a sense of direction when you are feeling like you are all over the place.

When you are struggling to bring peace and order to your internal environment, try putting your external environment in order first. The feeling you gain from it will translate into your inner world and you'll automatically start feeling more at ease with yourself.

EXERCISE

On a scale of 0 to 10 how cluttered is your environment (with 10 being extremely cluttered and 0 being not cluttered at all)? If your space is cluttered, then write down how it makes you feel. Do you feel overwhelmed by it, does it make you uneasy, etc.?

Are you satisfied with your physical environment? If no, then what can you do to improve your physical environment?

Are you holding on to items that you no longer like or need but you have to keep them because you spent money on them or because someone you cared about gave them to you? Note down the names of 5-10 such items. How does it feel to have such items around? Do they evoke positive feelings in you or they are a source of negative energy that leaves you feeling uneasy?

When it comes to these items that don't serve you any more can you give them away or put them to alternative use? Note down who you can give them to or how you can use them for alternative purposes.

Spend 10 minutes decluttering your space. You can pick a corner and declutter only that space. Get rid of 2 things you don't use anymore. Write down here how you felt after doing this exercise. Complete this exercise before moving on to the next section. You won't realize just how powerful it is until you try it out for yourself.

Note down all the feelings that came up for you during the process and after you completed the task. If you felt great, then add 10 minutes of decluttering to your daily schedule. It is one of the most effective ways of keeping your space in order and also an act of confronting your inner self through the medium of your external environment.

On a scale of 0-10, rate how clean your space is with 10 being extremely clean and 0 being extremely dirty. If you are not satisfied with the cleanliness of your space, then write down how you can improve the situation. Look into systems and methods that will help you create an easy-to-follow cleaning routine. If possible, you can also consider hiring help and paying someone else for it.

If cleaning is something you struggle with, then I would highly recommend reading the book *A Monk's Guide to a Clean House and Mind* by Shoukei Matsumoto. It is an extremely powerful book that may help transform your attitude and outlook towards cleaning. Maintaining a clean physical space is extremely important for maintaining internal hygiene. When you keep your space clean, you also polish your thoughts and emotions.

4

MASTERING YOUR INNER WORLD

"Take charge of your inner world by destroying the limitations caused by the outer distractions."

— HIRAL NAGDA

Your inner world creates and maintains the blueprint that dictates all your experiences in the outer world. Think about this – when you are in a good mood, it seems as if the entire world is joyful and happy. On the other hand, when you are in a bad mood, it seems as if every person you meet is grumpy and grouchy. Somehow the world outside has the ability to mirror our inner world to an unprecedented level of accuracy.

In the last chapter, I talked about intentionally organizing and optimizing your environment to support the kind of life you want to live. I covered the topic of working on your external environment first because making changes on the outside is often a lot easier than bringing about inner change.

Also, when you make changes in your external environment the results are concrete and clearly visible. Changes in the internal environment are often a lot more subtle and can often be hard to decipher. For instance, you don't always know the level of mental fortitude you have or that you have developed until you come-to-face with an extremely challenging situation and successfully overcome it.

While changes in the external environment are crucial for creating a congenial and harmonious atmosphere for our true self to thrive, it is through inner transformation that you will reach your highest potential in life. Your thoughts and emotions are part of your inner world. The outer world impacts it to a certain extent but without the right attitude, even the most harmonious outer atmosphere won't help you grow and reach your highest potential.

If you don't like your results in the external world, then you have to dive deep into your inner world. This book is called Emotional Regulation Skills but your thoughts and emotions are not problems to be dealt with. To thrive in life, you must get rid of the idea that certain thoughts or emotions are problematic. My goal with this book is not to teach you how to shut down those parts of yourself that society and other people have told you are undesirable.

There was a time in my life when I used to think the same way – that I need to shut down all "negative" thinking and constantly be in an elated happy mood. Life doesn't work like that. As humans, we are here to experience the full spectrum of what it means to be truly human. No emotion or thought is undesirable. Every emotion and every thought arises from a part of us that is seeking to be heard. We have to acknowledge all parts of us instead of trying to embrace only those parts that we believe are undesirable and abandon the ones we think are undesirable.

Through this book, I want to help you embrace yourself fully. The goal is not just to master your emotions and conquer your thoughts but to gain mastery over yourself. You automatically master your thoughts and emotions when you master yourself as they are parts of you. You must never treat them as separate from your Self. When you apply approaches to embrace and master all aspects of your being, your life transforms so deeply and intensely that you'll be amazed by who you have become even in a relatively short amount of time.

GIVE UP JUDGMENT

Socrates famously said, "The unexamined life is not worth living." (Socrates, n.d.) Indeed, you have to understand and examine your life very closely in order to gain mastery over it and over yourself. Make note here – the keyword is "understanding." In order to truly understand you must give up all judgment.

For me, one of the most empowering things has been to realize that everyone in the world has the same struggles as me. Most of the things we struggle with are human struggles. So if the alarm bell goes off and you keep putting it on snooze, it isn't just you. When you finally wake up, you say to yourself, "I am such a loser. I can't even wake up on time."

When you think it is just you who has these struggles, you start assuming there is something wrong with you but there is not a single person on the planet who hasn't done this or thought the same thing at some point. Always keep in mind that we are only looking at an external visage that other people are showing us. It is a carefully curated image of how someone wants to be seen and what they are allowing others to see. You don't know what someone's internal struggles are.

It may seem like highly productive and materially successful people have everything figured out but there isn't a single person in the world who isn't struggling with something. You can only be highly functional – perfection is an illusion. The only thing that separates the go-getters from the rest is that the former have trained themselves to take action and do what needs to be done irrespective of how they are feeling or all the doubts and fears that are plaguing them.

Yes, there isn't a single person on this planet who doesn't have some kind of fear or doubt. You can never get rid of them completely. You can only train yourself to act in spite of them.

Self-acceptance is the key to self-love. Self-transformation is enabled only through radical self-love. You have to embrace all parts of yourself if you want to love yourself fully, and, hence, transform yourself to be the person you have always wanted to be. It's all in your own hands. A lot of the labels that you have given yourself are not your own perceptions. They are labels and ideas that other people put upon you. Our early childhood experience dictates how we show up in life as an adult.

If your caregivers told you, "You are not good at this or that." It is only an idea. It is their perception of you. You heard it so many times that you decided to accept it as your truth. Since you accepted something as your truth, it became a part of your identity. From now on, I want you to start questioning every limiting belief you have. If you find yourself saying things like, "I am such an idiot" "I can't get anything right" – pause for a moment if what you are saying is really the truth. What evidence do you have to prove that the label or judgment you are subjecting yourself to is actually true? What are the counterarguments that oppose this idea?

I always say that the most important quality a person needs to develop is self-awareness. You have to start looking deep into your soul and being to start understanding yourself.

Don't accept any idea that doesn't serve you – question it, dissect it, and eventually, you'll be ready to discard it. What doesn't serve you should not have any place in your life.

Curate your thoughts, your emotions, your attitudes, and your outlook like you were responsible for maintaining the most beautiful garden in the world. It's true anyway – paradise is within you and so is hell. We create our own private heaven or hell depending upon the thoughts and emotions we choose to hold on to. Knowing it's all a choice is an extremely empowering realization. If you have chosen something you don't like, then you also have the power to choose differently now.

EXERCISE

Complete the following sentences with whatever negative beliefs or ideas come up in your mind. Don't think too much – the response that comes up immediately is essentially your programming.

I am terrible at

I can never do

I am such a/an

I hate myself when

I feel stupid when

I doubt that I am/I would

I always mess up

I struggle with

I will never be good at

Now, I want you to take a separate sheet of paper and write down each statement on top of it. Divide the page into two columns – write down on top "evidence" and "counter-evidence." In the first column write down all the evidence you have that proves the statement is correct. In the second column, write down why the statement is incorrect. Think of all those times when you did something that proves the statement is incorrect. Note down all the logical reasons why the statement is totally unfounded. Do it for all the statements. By the end of this exercise, you'll be surprised by the results.

A lot of things that we allow ourselves to believe are at best extremely faulty arguments that aren't grounded in reality at all. Logically working through these statements by weighing the evidence against the counter-evidence exposes how shoddy these beliefs are. Most of them aren't your own at all but ideas and beliefs you acquired from other people while growing up. They aren't a reflection of who you are but of the limited understanding that the person who transmitted these ideas to you had.

They believed certain things to be true about this world and of themselves, they projected those beliefs onto you. For instance, if they believed they can't do something, they'd tell you it can't be done. At some point, you started believing their words because repetition has that kind of power. If anything is repeated often enough, the mind starts accepting it as the truth. This is also why affirmations are so effective.

We can break down negative programming by constantly repeating new empowering beliefs.

Also, I am sure you didn't find it hard to come up with sentences to complete each one of the phrases. Trust me, it isn't just you. Every single person can fill the above questionnaire with ease because there is no one in this world who isn't grappling with some kind of doubt, insecurity or limiting beliefs. In life, we never truly arrive. No matter how far we have come, there is always another level at which we can play the game of life which requires us to advance even further and become an even finer version of ourselves.

Challenges are an essential part of life. The only thing that changes as you grow and become more is the way you deal with these challenges. The things that used to debilitate you previously become easy to tackle. At the same time, you have newer opportunities for growth in the form of new challenges you must overcome. There are infinite levels at which the game of life can be played. You can either look at it as something tragic or rejoice in the realization that the process of life is immensely dynamic and the opportunities for growth within just one human life are infinite.

YOUR THOUGHTS REVEAL A LOT ABOUT YOUR INNER AND OUTER WORLD

Your thoughts are like waves of an ocean – they arise and subside of their own accord. Don't try to hold on to them too tightly by dissecting and analyzing them. It will only frustrate and annoy you. Instead, your focus should be on witnessing them. Hold on to the ones that serve you and let go of the ones that aren't aligned with your highest good.

Our thoughts are strongly influenced by our external environment and by the company we keep. At the same time, our external environment and the company we are keeping are reflections of our internal framework that was established while growing up.

For instance, if you grew up in a highly dysfunctional family where your needs were hardly ever acknowledged and met, you may have anger issues and other emotional/behavioral problems. You'll attract people who are similar to you and you will constantly find yourself in environments that are aligned with the beliefs you have about the world.

So let us say you believe the world is full of jerks. You will constantly find yourself in the company of jerks. In life, we can never have more than what we believe we deserve. If you believe that living in a ramshackle house is all you deserve, then you simply won't be able to get yourself to be in a beautiful and luxurious house. Our beliefs and internal frameworks dictate every single experience of life.

At the same time, once you realize how the faulty programming of your internal world is holding you back and you start taking substantial steps to transform your reality, the people who are in your immediate environment won't like it at all. They will judge you, say harsh things to you, and will try to hold you back. It's not like they are bad people.

Most people aren't really thinking about their actions – they just act. And the reason why people engage in this kind of behavior is because you making improvements to your life often makes others uncomfortable. It holds a mirror to them and since they are not ready to make those same kinds of changes for whatever reason, they will be harsh and critical towards you in other to discourage you.

This is why you must constantly re-evaluate and reassess whether your peer group is holding you back in life or it is helping you make substantial progress in the direction of your goals. If you are constantly surrounded by pessimistic and negative people, then you will also become afflicted by such thoughts. It is also possible that your peer group may have served you at one point but that same group isn't aligned with who you are right now.

Most people are not growing and leveling up in life. If growth and being the highest version of yourself are priorities for you, then you must be willing to let go of people who are not aligned with who you are and where you want to go. Trust that nature abhors a vacuum. You will definitely meet new people who are better aligned with who you are and where you want to go.

I know I talked at length about the importance of surrounding yourself with the right people in the previous chapter but this topic is so important that I couldn't help reiterating it here as well. The other aspect that we must look at is that your thoughts arise from different parts of you. There are parts of you that "nurture" you and there are those parts of you that "protect" you. They are like your internal mother and father.

The aspect of you that is a protector has internalized the voice of the primary caregiver who was most critical of you. This voice chides you and is constantly cautioning you not to do certain things. Whenever you have a negative experience that causes you pain, it gets stored in your subconscious mind. If you encounter a similar situation in the future, the protector warns you again. For instance, if you had several failed relationships and you meet a new person with whom you are exploring the possibility of exploring a new relationship, the protector may constantly be on guard waiting for things to go wrong because that's what happened last time.

The protector may also caution you against trusting this new person and may try to talk you out of forging a relationship with them. Instead of rejecting the protector, you must acknowledge all the "negative" thoughts and understand that they come from a part of you which is seeking to be heard. All parts of you want the best for you. The nurturer encourages you and helps you move forward while the protector tries its best to prevent the recurrence of painful experiences from the past.

Your goal is to strengthen the voice of the nurturer while also hearing and acknowledging the protector. Let the protector know that you understand their intentions, acknowledge their concerns, and appreciate what they are doing for you. Once you do this, you'll feel immediate relief. Those "negative" thoughts that were bothering you so much would cease to have so much power and influence over you.

Pain comes from rejection. When you don't hear and acknowledge all aspects of yourself, those parts would scream louder for your attention. Give up this idea that some parts of you are desirable and others are not. All parts of you are desirable. Both "negative" and "positive" thoughts are essential to the human experience. Whatever we reject becomes even more powerful. If you embrace that all those "bad" thoughts that come up every now and then are just thoughts arising out of different parts of you, and you seek to understand the pain, frustration, and suffering this part is experiencing, those thoughts would cease to bother you.

Sometimes I feel extremely angry at my mother to the point that I want to hurt her emotionally and psychologically. Society tells us that we should never have such thoughts towards anyone, definitely not toward the person who has given birth to us. The problem with this kind of thinking is that it denies our humanness. If people were brutally honest, we'd know for sure that there isn't a single person on the planet who doesn't feel the urge to hurt another person at one point or another.

Most of the time, this desire or instinct to hurt another arises out of our own woundedness. In my case, I had an extremely difficult childhood. I didn't have the kind of childhood where my parents would be constantly doting on me. Instead, I felt lonely, unheard, and unacknowledged growing up. It seemed like I and my needs just didn't matter. As a child, I wasn't able to voice how I felt. Even if I tried to express myself, I was told to shut up. This created a lot of inner frustration and anger.

Once I started understanding that the part of me which wants to hurt my mother is really the wounded inner child whose needs weren't met, I can have more empathy for myself. I am also able to embrace the experience of having such thoughts and emotions arise in me as something "normal." It is perfectly normal to feel the way I do at times because of the kind of life experiences I had. Now, I am not making excuses for bad behavior or for actually hurting someone else. Having thoughts like that when you have been wounded and hurt is normal but as a human being, you have the choice to embrace the thoughts and emotions without acting on them.

Embracing your "negative" thoughts and emotions by trying to understand the parts of you that have been wounded and hurt can help you forge a deeper more meaningful relationship with yourself. The most important relationship in life is not with anyone else but with your own self. You must invest in this relationship because it is one relationship that is guaranteed to bring huge returns throughout your life. The relationship you have with yourself sets the ground for your relationships with other people. You can never have a better relationship with anyone else without first having an incredible relationship with yourself.

You have to be there for yourself. You must hear, acknowledge, and fully embrace who you are. All parts of you make you who you are. There isn't a single part of you that is undesirable, unwanted or bad. There are parts of you that are concerned for you that want to protect you. By acknowledging the thoughts and emotions which arise from them (which society labels as "negative" or "bad") you are embracing yourself fully. All parts of you are beautiful. It is our real and perceived imperfections that make us unique. The wide spectrum of emotions and thoughts we experience throughout a lifetime defines our humanness. For a truly fulfilling and rewarding life, we have to be completely at home with ourselves – with all parts of us.

Once I fully started embracing the "negative" thoughts and feelings I had towards my mother, I started understanding that part of me which was deeply wounded. As I healed this part of me by understanding its needs and trying to meet it as best as possible now as an adult, I was also able to have compassion for my mother. I understood that she was doing the best that she was capable of but her own dysfunctional childhood made her the type of person she was. I let go of my desire to seek some kind of redemption for the childhood I never had.

I can't go back in time but I can use the challenging and painful experiences of my life to become better in the here and now. The greatest secret to a successful life is to master the art of turning your weaknesses into strengths, your pain, and challenges into blessings. My relationship with my mother isn't perfect and it is never going to be but I am at peace with my life – that's what matters!

EXERCISE

For the next three days, write down all the "negative" thoughts and feelings you are experiencing. You can create a dedicated journal for this practice and carry it with you everywhere. Whenever a negative thought or emotion comes up, write it down immediately. Seek to really hear yourself. Write down which part of you is trying to communicate with you and what they are trying to say.

For instance, that part of you which tells you not to get on a stage and give a speech may be trying to protect you from the pain and embarrassment you faced a long time ago when you spoke on stage as a child. Hear that part of you and say to yourself, "I hear you." Embrace the thought and feeling fully instead of trying to suppress it or run away from it. Very soon, it will go away on its own very much like how a wave arises and subsides of its own accord on the seabed.

5

YOUR EXTERNAL SUPPORT SYSTEM

"Finally, be kind to yourself and have a good support system."

— NIKKI DELOACH

Having a reliable support system is absolutely essential for effectively managing our emotions and thoughts. There are two types of support systems: external and internal. Your external support system consists of friends, family, mentors, therapists, and others who are there for you when you need help. Your internal support comprises your ability to self-soothe.

You can't always rely on others to give you what you want. Even if someone wanted to, it really isn't possible for any person in the world to be there for us a hundred percent of the time. Of course, we should express our needs to others in an authentic and honest way. That's how a great relationship is built. But we must also always have the ability to self-soothe.

In this chapter, we'll focus on external support systems for now. In the next chapter, I will teach you how you can build and strengthen your internal support system. Again, I want to emphasize that no thought or emotion is "bad." Whatever we suppress becomes even more potent at the subconscious level and continues to bother us in ways we may not consciously understand.

We have to be willing to accept, acknowledge, and face all the emotions that arise inside. No thought or feeling is bad – thoughts and feelings just are. They are there to help us experience life fully. Life can never be fully experienced without embracing the full spectrum of emotions and thoughts. Don't suppress or reject what comes up. Instead, seek to dive deep into yourself to learn more.

When you have the right kind of internal and external system, it becomes easy to manage all our thoughts and emotions without suppression. Without the right kind of internal and external support system, you may look for help at all the wrong places or you will seek to numb yourself. Hence, having a strong support system isn't a luxury but an absolute necessity for living a meaningful and fulfilling life.

GETTING TO THE ROOT OF THINGS

I cannot emphasize enough the fact that we are the sum total of our life experiences. How our primary caregivers responded to us in early life sets the stage for all our close personal relationships throughout life including the relationship we have with ourselves. If your childhood was fraught with trauma, you will have difficulty managing your emotions and thoughts. This is nothing to be ashamed of. It is a natural response to unmet needs and to the feeling of "not being seen."

Even if you had a fairly happy childhood where your needs were met and you felt seen, chances are there were certain parts of yourself you weren't able to express. Maybe you were chastised every time you expressed anger. From those experiences, you learned that anger is "bad" so now you deny the emotion of anger whenever it arises as a natural response to certain situations.

Again, no emotion is bad. Every emotion is there to help us fully experience life as a human being. Anger is a natural and very human response to situations we find unpleasant or where we feel threatened. Anger doesn't go away when it is suppressed. The only way to release it (and any difficult emotion for that matter) is by fully experiencing it. Keep in mind that acting out of anger and fully experiencing the feeling of anger are two completely different things altogether. I am not asking you to do the former. Acting in anger or out of anger is not healthy and can severely damage your personal relationships.

I am suggesting that you acknowledge your anger and look within to find out what it is trying to communicate to you. For instance, when I was little my mother would often shout at me for no fault of my own. She was frustrated with her own life and her marriage. Since I was a child, it was easy for her to take it out on me. I am not saying that she was doing it intentionally but there is no denying that these screaming episodes caused considerable damage to me and the experience of being shouted upon lived with me long through my adult life.

When my mother would scream at me for no reason, I would feel very angry. I also felt violated because I was unfairly being treated badly. As anger seethed in me, I tried confronting her a few times asking her what exactly had I done wrong. The truth was she didn't know why she was behaving the way she was. My questions would only exacerbate her frustration and anger. She would shout back saying, "How dare you ask me such a question! Shut up or I'll give you something to cry about."

From this experience, my inner child learned that anger was something "bad." I started suppressing all my negative feelings because I was afraid of upsetting my mother and making her anger even worse. I often walked on eggshells trying very hard not to upset her. No matter how hard I tried, she would find one reason or another to shout at me and scold me. I started suppressing my needs because asking her to meet any of them meant trouble.

From my childhood experiences, I learned that certain emotions and thoughts were "bad." I felt guilty whenever I felt angry or I wanted to say something nasty to my mother or anyone else whose behavior made me feel hurt. I also internalized the idea that my needs didn't matter. I became an over-giving excessively selfless person. The problem with being such a person is that it never comes from a place of authenticity. It is a classic trauma-based response.

Every person has needs and it is our right to expect others to meet them. Of course, we can't demand that others give us what we want – we can only politely ask for it. Some people won't give us what we want but there are more than 8 billion people on the planet. There certainly are many people in this world who are eager to give us what we want. We have to make ourselves good receivers by accepting graciously what is given to us and by also learning to politely ask for our needs to be met.

Irrespective of the kind of childhood you had, we all need to heal the inner child. Most people think of trauma only as something very extreme like being sexually or physically abused but trauma is a very individual experience. Trauma is any kind of mental, emotional, and spiritual scar that needs to be healed.

Maybe you had fantastically supportive parents but you had a few episodes in school where you were mocked by other students and that caused you to suppress certain parts of yourself. It is your job to find out which parts of your inner child you have suppressed or shut down. This is what lies at the root of all our problems with managing thoughts and emotions.

The thoughts and emotions we perceive as problems are simply parts of us that are seeking to be heard and validated. There is no shortcut to building thought and emotional regulation skills without healing the parts of us that have been suppressed and wounded in some way.

EXERCISE

Write down all those thoughts and emotions that you currently perceive as undesirable. If you need more space, feel free to use additional sheets of paper to note down everything. You want to be as thorough as possible.

Pick up one thought/emotion that bothers you the most and dive deep into how your problems with it started. I would recommend that you set aside around an hour to be completely by yourself. Create a relaxing atmosphere for yourself by practicing deep breathing (breathe deeply in on a count of 1-2-3-4 and breathe out gradually on a count of 1-2-3-4).

You can also play some relaxing music in the background and light some incense to help yourself relax. When you are ready close your eyes and go back to a time when you started internalizing the idea that the particular thought/emotion is bad. Try to recall the incident fully in as much detail as possible. When you are ready, open your eyes and write down everything you found out.

If no clear memory emerges, then simply observe whatever comes up. When someone has experienced severe trauma, they may not be able to recall anything at all as the mind may prevent them from recalling it so they don't have to relive the severe trauma. If this is happening with you, then just be patient with yourself. Observe whatever feelings, thoughts, and ideas come up and note those down.

Close your eyes and observe where in your body, you feel these thoughts/emotions. Unexpressed suppressed emotions get stored in the different parts of the body. They often manifest as aches and pains or other maladies. By scanning your body mentally with closed eyes, you'll be able to identify where exactly you feel these suppressed thoughts and emotions. When you are ready, open your eyes and note down your findings.

Now, go back to that incident from where the suppression began. In case you can't recall the actual incident, then just allow yourself to simply "be" with whatever is coming up. Become mindful of all the sensations that are happening in the body. Observe how the suppressed emotions have been stored in the body. If you are able to replay the incident in your mind, then relive it fully. Observe how you felt in that exact moment – where in your body you felt all the emotions and thoughts. As you are reliving the situation, instead of suppressing how you are feeling, embrace your thoughts and emotions fully.

Say to yourself, "I acknowledge you. I accept you. All your thoughts and feelings are justified." Repeat this sentence to yourself as many times as needed. Be there for yourself. Whatever you needed at the time from others, you can now give to yourself. Give yourself the gift of understanding and acceptance.

This is a very powerful exercise. You can repeat it as many times as needed. I would recommend that you do it for all the thoughts and emotions you have suppressed. In order to gain mastery over your mind and your emotions, you have to first experience them fully without the seeking to suppress anything. By simply being fully present with them, you initiate the healing process.

YOUR EXTERNAL SUPPORT SYSTEM

We all need people around us who understand and support us. I am sure you have at least one person in your life right now or you had someone like that in the past. If you feel there is no one in your life who understands and supports you, then there is a lot of work to be done. Keep in mind, the people we surround ourselves with are always similar to us in some way.

If you don't have anyone in your life right now who wants to be there for you, then most likely you are surrounding yourself with people who are wounded and preoccupied with themselves. The solution lies in healing yourself. I'll suggest that you focus on building your internal support system for now. As you heal and evolve, in the external world, people will appear who will be aligned with who you would have become by then.

If you already have at least one person in your life who supports you and understands you, then I want to focus on how you can get the best out of that connection. When we are wounded and preoccupied with our own unmet needs, we don't communicate effectively. The other person may sincerely want to help us but people are not mind readers. We can't expect others to know our needs without us expressing them. I want to empower you with the skills you need to assert yourself and express your needs.

Your needs are important. You are important. You must learn to express what you want with clarity and honesty. That's how you will strengthen your external support system so others can help you in your journey the way you want to be helped. I am also going to share with you ideas for intentionally building and expanding your external support system.

EXPRESS YOUR NEEDS USING "I" STATEMENTS

What's the best way of making sure the other person won't do anything for you? Tell them how they never do anything for you – you'll pretty much be guaranteed that they won't do anything for you. Most of us are not taught how to communicate our needs effectively. We don't know how to express our difficult thoughts and emotions in a way that others would empathize with.

If you can relate, then don't despair. It isn't just you. Most people have no idea how to process and express whatever is bothering them. Chances are you were given the silent treatment or maybe your primary caregivers screamed at you every time you tried to express those thoughts and feelings. The good news is that effective clear communication is a skill that anyone can learn at any age.

You must also understand that we often overestimate how much time people spend thinking about us. The truth is we are all preoccupied with ourselves. One of the greatest life skills you can learn is the ability to not take things personally. Don't read too much into people's behavior and attribute meaning that isn't actually there.

If you want someone to do something for you, then you must ask for it clearly and honestly. Yes, there is always a 50% chance they won't do what you want but there is also a 50% chance that they may give you what you want. If you won't ask for what you want, then chances are almost null that you'll get exactly what you want.

So what exactly does it mean to be able to express your needs using "I" statements? Let us say you want to talk about how frustrated you are with work. You ask your spouse to listen to you – they start offering you solutions but that's not what you want. You just wanted them to validate your emotions and empathize with you. In the past, you would get frustrated and say things like, "You just don't understand me."

This statement sounds accusative. It would immediately make your spouse defensive – they were trying the best from their perspective. Even though they want to be there for you, they just don't know how. Feeling attacked isn't going to help redeem the situation much. Now, how about you employ a different approach and say to them, "Darling, I really want to vent about my tough day at work. I don't want to discuss solutions right now. I just want you to listen to me and empathize with me."

With this statement, you are telling them exactly what you want. There is no room for guesswork here. Most of the problems in relationships happen because people want the other person to read their mind. No one can do that. You have to maximize your chances of getting your needs met by clearly expressing exactly what it is you want from the other person. This is just one scenario but you can apply it to any situation.

These are the golden rules of effective communication:

- Use 'I" statements. "I would like you to..." "I would appreciate it if you..."
- Tell the other person exactly what they can do for you. Don't be demanding. Simply state what you want without pressurizing them to meet your needs.
- Explain how it will help you or how their doing what you want would add value to your life.
- When someone gives you what you want, be sure to express your gratitude. What gets rewarded, gets repeated!

BE WILLING TO HAVE DIFFICULT CONVERSATIONS

Most people shy away from difficult conversations. They suppress their emotions and needs until one day the lid blows off and they explode. Nothing good comes out of suppressing your own feelings and needs. You have to get comfortable being uncomfortable. Life is never fulfilling in the comfort zone. The more you step out of your comfort zone, the more you'll grow. The more you grow, the more fulfilling your life will be.

As I said earlier, when you state your needs, there is always a 50-50 chance it will be met but if you never state it, then chances are you'll never get what you want. I know how tough it can be to have these conversations, especially if you didn't grow up in a household where such communication was appreciated or engaged in. But now, as an adult, you are fully in charge of how you live your life. You deserve to have your needs met!

Very often I visualize initiating these difficult conversations as akin to jumping in a pool. I like to use Mel Robbins' five-second rule for taking action and beating procrastination (Robbins, 2017). So I just count 5-3-2-1 and do it. The more time you spend contemplating doing it, the more time your mind will have to talk you out of doing it. It is also painful to remain in such a state of limbo. You just need to give your-self an initial push like how you would do before jumping into the pool.

There is something incredibly freeing about being able to express your own truth even if the other person doesn't end up giving you what you want. The fact that you expressed what you wanted helps you feel liberated. Also, this kind of honest and open communication reveals to you who your true well-wishers are and who isn't truly there for you. The people who value you and love you will remain with you no matter what. They will try their best to meet your needs without sabotaging their own. But if you don't ask, the answer is always going to be "No."

EXERCISE

What is it that you want from others but you have never tried asking for it? Pick one thing that would make the greatest difference to your life right now and then commit to having that tough conversation. If that sounds too intimidating, then pick something where the stakes are pretty low. Ask for something that you don't care so much about but it would still be nice if you could have it.

As you gain practice and reap the benefits of your efforts, you'll want to repeat the process in other areas of your life where the stakes are higher and the outcome would make a tremendous difference to your life. If you find yourself procrastinating, visualize jumping into the swimming pool. Hold your breath, count till five and just do it!

After having the conversation, come back here and write down how you felt after having the conversation. I am sure you'll realize just how liberating it is to have such an open and honest conversation. Start turning this into a habit. Try to have an honest and open conversation with everyone who matters in your life.

SEEK OUT OTHERS WHO CAN HELP YOU

It is also a great idea to intentionally keep expanding your external support system by seeking those who have similar goals to you and others who can mentor you. How to do it practically? Thanks to the internet, it is easier than ever to meet people from all over the world with a few clicks of a button. You can find forums and support groups related to just about any topic. You can also meet people locally in clubs dedicated to a common interest. When you meet people with similar passions, interests, and struggles, chances are high they will understand you and you will be able to understand them.

It is also a good idea to work with or just be around coaches, mentors, therapists, and other experts from whom you can learn various skills. You can gain access to them by buying their books, attending courses, doing one-on-one sessions, etc. Yes, this will most likely require some kind of financial investment from your end but investing in yourself is one type of investment that always pays off great dividends. If you aren't sure, then start with books and free resources online like YouTube videos, podcasts, etc.

EXERCISE

In which area of your life do you need help right now? Look up online and offline groups, forums, etc. where you can meet others who have similar goals as you. Look up mentors, coaches, and experts in this area and start learning from them.

6

UNDERSTANDING NEEDS AND BOUNDARIES

"Boundaries define us. They define what is me and what is not me. A boundary shows me where I end and someone else begins, leading me to a sense of ownership. Knowing what I am to own and take responsibility for gives me freedom. Taking responsibility for my life opens up many different options. Boundaries help us keep the good in and the bad out."

— HENRY CLOUD

I decided to dedicate an entire chapter to boundary setting because this is an aspect of emotional regulation that often gets ignored. Emotional regulation is not about not having certain types of emotions or forcing yourself to feel certain emotions. Emotional regulation is about giving yourself a safe space to feel all your emotions irrespective of judgment and resistance.

Feeling your emotions by acknowledging, accepting, and even embracing them to a certain extent doesn't imply you have to act on them. This is where boundaries come into play. The boundaries you have with yourself and with others help you operate with awareness and self-control while you still maintain a safe space to feel the full spectrum of your emotional world.

As I always say, the key to emotional regulation is intense self-awareness. This same idea applies to boundary setting. You can set clear boundaries with others only when you know who you are, what you stand for, and what you want. Too many people are afraid to do this because they fear losing the relationship with the other person or upsetting others.

Trust me, no relationship is worth compromising with your boundaries for. You have the right to say "No." But you can say "no" with firmness and conviction only when you know what your own needs and priorities are. I'm not saying this is going to be easy. Once you start setting firm and clear boundaries, you'll certainly receive a lot of backlash from the people who benefitted from your lack of boundaries in the past.

You have to be prepared to be called "mean" and "selfish." Just know that being called "nice" is often not a compliment and certainly not something to be proud of. A lot of times it means you are allowing others to take from you whatever they want at the expense of your own needs and well-being. If you want to live a truly fulfilling life, you have to master the art of saying no. Your desire to care for yourself and your well-being must become stronger than your desire to be liked by others.

WHAT DOES IT MEAN TO HAVE STRONG BOUNDARIES?

I want to give you a definition that you can refer to which will help you assess how you are doing with establishing and maintaining personal boundaries. I would say a boundary is a real or perceived line around your property (including both your body/mind/soul and your material possessions in the external world) that should not be crossed under any circumstance.

We live in a society where having a fence around our physical property is the norm but no one teaches us how to have strong boundaries that protect our mind, body, and soul. In fact, there is a lot of guilt associated with boundary setting. A lot of people think that establishing boundaries makes them selfish. From a young age, this idea gets embedded in their psyche by teachers and parents who themselves lacked strong boundaries.

You are taught that to be "good," you must pander to other people's wishes even at the expense of your own mental, emotional, physical, and spiritual well-being. Hence, once you start setting boundaries as an adult, you encounter a lot of old programming that makes you think it is "bad" to have boundaries. Mastering the art of boundary setting requires a tremendous amount of unlearning. You have to let go of old ways of relating that are no longer serving you.

It is going to be very tough practicing emotional regulation skills if you are constantly allowing your desire to please others precedes over prioritizing your own needs and well-being. A lot of emotional issues people face in life is because they are constantly ignoring their own needs, desires, wants, and goals. Just because you are taught to live a certain way doesn't mean it is the right way to be or what's best for you.

Every time you do something and it just doesn't feel quite "right" in your gut, you know you are going against your nature and your needs. I am not talking about the kind of discomfort that comes from doing a difficult or challenging task – that may be painful but it leaves you feeling better about yourself. Every time you push your boundaries in order to grow and evolve into a higher version of yourself, the resultant satisfaction and self-esteem far outweigh the discomfort you experienced.

On the other hand, when you say yes to something that requires you to compromise your needs and your values, the experience leaves you feeling depleted and drained. If you keep denying your own needs and continue going against your core values, eventually, you'll build a huge reservoir of resentment and anger. It is only a matter of time before you'll blow up and experience rage toward the people you resent and are angry at.

Being a person with strong boundaries implies asserting your needs and pursuing your self-interest. I know that this is frowned upon by society. You are likely thinking, "Are you not asking me to be selfish by suggesting that I assert my needs and pursue my self-interests?" Valid question – I used to think the same way! It took me a long time to arrive at this understanding that looking after my own needs and protecting my personal boundaries doesn't make me selfish. Think of what happens when you say yes to someone else at the expense of your own self. You do what you think is right but internally, you start building resentment.

Also, most people don't say what they want because healthy communication is a skill that the majority never learn. Asserting your needs doesn't imply being mean and demanding. It means you tell others what they can do for you and then you give them the choice to give you what you need or not give it to you. Most people will never ask others what they want because they are too afraid of rejection. But think of it like this – if you never ask, chances are negligible that you'll ever receive what you want.

Even if you don't get what you want, at least you'll have the satisfaction of knowing you tried. Besides, you didn't have what you wanted in the first place so not having it after you have asked doesn't make you worse off. But what if you asked for something and you received it? Isn't it worth trying? After all, there is always at least a 50% chance that you may receive what you are asking for. If you don't ask, you'll likely never find out what you may have received by being vocal and upfront!

Asserting your needs comprises both asking for what you want from someone else and also for what you don't want them to do. A lot of times people have no idea that their actions, behavior, or words may be impacting us in the wrong way. Most people remain quiet and never express the truth about how they are feeling. This causes rifts in relationships while also having a negative impact on overall personal satisfaction.

On the other hand, telling others how they can make you more comfortable and at ease in their presence will help you build deeper connections with others. Being able to say you don't like something or don't want something is one of the most important boundary-setting skills that you must acquire if you want to live a fulfilling life.

EXERCISE

What are the needs that you are ignoring right now?

How often do you stay "yes" to things you don't want to do?
Why do you think you do it?

What is preventing you from saying how you truly feel about
the thing you are being asked to do? What are you afraid of?
What do you fear will happen if you say "no"?

Are you compromising with your core values to meet other people's needs and demands? What are these core values that you are compromising on right now?

How do you feel when you say "yes" to a demand or request you don't want to meet? Think of the last time you did it and try to recall everything you felt in your body. In which part of your body did you feel the maximum discomfort? Describe that feeling in as much detail as possible. Next time, you find yourself saying "yes" to something you'd much rather say "no" to observe what happens in your body and make note of it.

Is it easy for you to tell others what you want from them? Write down the reasons that prevent you from asking others to give you what you would like to have.

Do you feel your needs and boundaries are important or do you feel you must keep "sacrificing" putting your own needs on the back burner in order to serve others?

Go back to your childhood and write down how your primary caregivers responded to you every time you said "no" to something you didn't want to do. How did it make you feel? What was the message that you received and internalized from their response to you?

_____

_____

_____

_____

_____

_____

Go back to your childhood and write down how your primary caregivers responded to you every time you asserted your boundaries by telling them what is acceptable to you and what is not. How did it make you feel? What was the message that you received and internalized from their response to you?

_____

_____

_____

_____

_____

_____

UNDERSTANDING YOUR RESPONSES TO THE EXERCISE ABOVE

I hope you have completed the exercises from the previous section. If not, I would urge you to go back and complete them. This section will help you dive deeper into your responses so you can understand why you are the way you are but reading it without an understanding of your own behavior and mindset patterns won't help you much.

As I always say, transformation happens through action. Reading and absorbing new information is important but it has real value only when we implement the wisdom we have extracted from the words we have read or heard.

The most fascinating thing about psychology is that it helps us understand why we are the way we are. The answer can often be traced back to early life. Our early childhood experiences lay down the foundation for how we show up in the world and interact with it as adults.

The stability of a child's early life has profound effects on physical and mental health, and unstable parent-child relationships, as well as abuse, can lead to behavioral disorders and increased mortality and morbidity from a wide variety of common diseases later in life (McEwen, 2003).

If you have trouble acknowledging and catering to your needs as an adult, you actually learned this behavior pattern long ago from your relationship with your primary caregivers. This isn't about blame but about understanding. When we understand how our behavior pattern was formed, we realize that most of the actions we engage in are learned responses.

If we can learn dysfunctional behavior patterns, then we can also unlearn them. I'm not saying it is easy but it is certainly worthwhile and most definitely possible. You can train yourself to think, act, respond, and behave like the person you have always wanted to be. You have the right to live life on your own terms and be whoever you wish to be.

Going back to the subject of early childhood experiences, if you grew up feeling like your needs don't matter, you would continue the same pattern into your adult connections. To change things, you must become conscious of what your needs and values are. Living a fulfilling life does require intense self-awareness. Expressing and asserting your needs effectively is a learnable skill but to get the most out of it, you must be aware of your values and goals. Who are you? Who you do you want to be? What are the goals you want to accomplish right now?

When you know the answer to the above questions (at least with some degree of clarity) asserting yourself in your relationships with others becomes simpler. A lot of times people don't express their needs because they fear rejection. Maybe you expressed your needs to your parents as a child and they responded with anger and violence.

Their response taught you that expressing your needs was dangerous and it should be avoided as much as possible. As an adult, if you express your needs most people won't respond in such an extreme way but the fear of such an intense reaction has become internalized in your system.

The solution lies in becoming self-aware. You have to get past stories of who you think you are and adopt new ways of being. In other words, you need to shift your mindset and start reprogramming yourself by building a skill set that you could not acquire from your early childhood environment. Trust me, there are many people in this world who would love to give you what you want.

You just need to identify who these people are and express your needs to them. Of course, there will be times when you won't receive what you ask for. When that happens, you must respect other people's boundaries and always remember that asking others for what you want doesn't obligate them to give it to you.

It simply gives them an opportunity to bestow upon you a gift that you truly want but as sovereign beings they have the right to refuse it. You don't have to force anyone to give you what you want. Don't get fixated on people – just know that for every person who says no to you, there is someone in the world who would eagerly say yes.

You just need to keep doing what's best for you – openly and honestly expressing your needs. Even if you get rejected, you won't die of it. As a child, conforming to your environment by suppressing your own needs was essential to your survival but you are no longer that child. You are an adult who has the power to remove themselves from any environment that isn't suitable for them. You also have the power to recreate your environment and your social circle.

Besides, every time you do get your needs met, you are reinforcing a new pattern – a new way of being. With every positive experience, you are reprogramming yourself in a positive way. This brings you closer to your goals and to the person you want to be. Also, there is something incredibly liberating about expressing your own truth. When you speak out, you feel free even if the idea of speaking out was frightening initially. You also have the conviction and the satisfaction that you tried your best irrespective of the result that you get. However, once you start doing this, you'll be surprised by how frequently people are actually eager to give you what you want, especially those who truly love you and care for you.

STOP OVER-GIVING

We live in a world where we are constantly bombarded by this idea of giving, giving, giving... Most people have become really good at giving but there is an essential life skill they never learned – how to receive! So let me ask you this – how comfortable are you with receiving? Do you receive heartfelt gifts (whether material items, time, energy, compliments, etc.) gracefully or with guilt? Do you feel you deserve what you receive or you feel unworthy of them?

Most people don't get in life what they want because deep inside they feel unworthy of it. If that sounds like you, then I want to say to you, "It is okay to feel this way!" We must acknowledge and embrace all our feelings, emotions, and thoughts. They are telling us where we have been, what we have learned, how we operate in the world according to the programming we have received. At the same time, we don't have to act on these feelings, thoughts, and emotions. We can retrain ourselves to show up differently in the world and in our relationships – including in our relationship with ourselves.

You are not good at receiving because no one taught you how to receive gracefully. If you are always the person who is giving, then you are not honoring the natural ebb and flow of life. Harmony and balance are the core principles upon with nature herself operates. When we refuse to receive with grace and gratitude, we are actually causing an imbalance in the natural flow of life. This is why we end up feeling so uneasy when we receive a beautiful gift someone wanted to give us. The other person also feels deprived and uneasy because they were stripped off an opportunity for doing something good for another human being.

EXERCISE

How do you feel when someone wants to give you something?

How do you respond when someone compliments you?

Do you ask for help when you need it?

How do you feel when you receive something you ask for?
Do you feel worthy of it or do you feel guilty?

Do you apologize excessively every time you ask for help
and when you feel someone may be inconveniencing themselves to give you what you need?

HOW TO BE A GOOD RECEIVER

Like most things in life, being a good receiver is a skill that you develop through consistent practice. It doesn't matter how bad you have been at it so far, if you want to change, then nothing can prevent you from becoming an excellent receiver. Yes, we are talking about balance here. You want to be good at both giving and receiving. You must do good to others but you must also allow others to do good unto you.

So here's how you do it:

When someone offers you a compliment, don't sabotage it by explaining how their words are not true. It is akin to rejecting a beautifully wrapped present by throwing it back in the giver's face. Neither the giver nor the receiver feels enriched by such an experience. Instead, just say "thank you" with a smile. You also don't need to compliment them back. A compliment that is given to the other person as a response to their original compliment doesn't come across as genuine. Instead, just enjoy their gift. If you want to give them a genuine compliment, then reserve it for later. In this moment, just allow yourself to bask in the glory of the wonderful gift they have given you.

Use "I" statement to ask others for help. "I need..." "I want..." "I would appreciate it if you would..." "I would love it if you would..." Get rid of this idea that you are inconveniencing them by asking them for help. If they can't give you what you need, let them be the one to decide this. By asserting your needs, you are giving them a chance to do something for you. Trust that you are worthy of it and that doing something for you is not an obligation but something beautiful, pleasurable, and joyous for another human being.

Don't apologize excessively when someone does something for you. You are worthy of their time and energy. Start believing that they are just as enriched by the experience of giving you something you need as you have been enriched by it. A heartfelt "thank you" and a genuine appreciation for their efforts is all you need to give them in return.

EXERCISE

Ask someone to do something for you. Be polite, clear, and assertive. For example, if you feel overwhelmed preparing and serving dinner, then today ask your partner if they would help you in the process. Use I statements like, "Honey, I would really love it if you would help me chop the vegetables for dinner." "I would appreciate it if you would help me set the table."

Whatever it is you want, just ask for it clearly and when you receive it, trust that you absolutely deserve what you are receiving. If by any chance, you are met with a refusal, don't take it personally. When someone refuses you something it simply means they are unable to give you what you want right now. It doesn't diminish your value as a human being. However, most of the time, people will be happy to give you what you want provided you state your needs clearly and with "I" statements.

If you are really afraid of refusal, start by asking for small favors and when people give you what you want. Build up your muscle from there and then move on to the things that would really make a huge difference to your life.

7

HANDLING INTENSE EMOTIONS AND EMOTIONAL BREAKDOWNS

"Your emotions make you human. Even the unpleasant ones have a purpose. Don't lock them away. If you ignore them, they just get louder and angrier."

— SABAA TAHIR

In this chapter, I want to give you practical tools for handling emotions. I want you to have a toolkit with you for times of intense emotional turmoil. They are indeed part of the human experience. Building emotional regulation skills doesn't imply you will never experience intense emotions again. It is all about how you handle these intense emotions and your emotional world in general.

I have said this before and I will say it again. All your emotions are important. There is no such thing as an undesirable emotion. As human beings, we must allow ourselves to experience the full spectrum of emotions. It takes a great deal of maturity to sit with uncomfortable emotions, simply feeling and witnessing them. The harder you try to reject something, the stronger it will come back at you. The emotions you reject never go away. They simply slip deep inside your subconscious mind from where they continue to impact your mind, emotions, and behavior.

WHAT ARE INTENSE EMOTIONS?

That being said, there is a difference between experiencing intense emotions and having emotional breakdowns. Experiencing intense emotions implies undergoing a state of feeling powerful emotions. This includes both positive and negative emotions. You can feel just as overwhelmed with love and joy as you can be with anger and hate. Intense emotions can be overpowering and overwhelming in the sense that they can negatively impact your ability to function in daily life.

Intense emotions often trigger a fight-or-flight response leaving us with trepidation, sweating, and a palpitating heart. We all experience intense emotions every now and then. They can happen as a response to specific events, situations, people, and places. They can also result from a build-up of stress over time. In some cases, when a person perpetually and constantly experiences intense emotions to the extent that it becomes debilitating and dysfunctional, there can be other major issues lurking under the surface.

For instance, when a person perpetually and regularly responds to situations and events with emotions that are not in proportion to the event and situation itself, it can be a sign of depression, bipolar disorder, ADHD and other mental health conditions. There are also genetic factors that can make certain individuals more prone to intense emotions than others (Bergland, 2015). Hence, we can't always say that someone who perpetually experiences intense emotions has some kind of mental health condition. It can also just be a genetic predisposition that makes them a very emotionally intense person.

WHAT IS AN EMOTIONAL BREAKDOWN?

An emotional breakdown is a period of extreme emotional distress that causes severe disruption to a person's daily life. Emotional breakdowns can occur in the aftermath of a traumatic event or as a result of mental and emotional suppression over an extended period of time.

When a person is having an emotional breakdown they may lose their appetite, have debilitating anxiety, suffer from insomnia, and struggle to concentrate on even the simplest tasks of daily life. These are only some of the key characteristics of an emotional breakdown and not all of them.

During an emotional breakdown, people often feel like their life is spiraling out of control. They also find it really hard to control themselves. This can lead to abrupt spells of crying, shouting, screaming, angry outbursts, etc. They struggle to contain and manage their emotions. Everything feels out of control and it becomes hard and sometimes impossible to operate in daily life.

When a person is having an emotional breakdown, they may withdraw from all social interactions. They may also struggle with basic self-care like taking a shower, fixing a meal for themselves, etc. It is very important to have compassion for oneself when one is undergoing an emotional breakdown. It is also advisable to seek professional help, especially if the breakdown continues for extended periods of time.

THE DIFFERENCE BETWEEN EXPERIENCING INTENSE EMOTIONS AND HAVING AN EMOTIONAL BREAKDOWN

The key difference between experiencing intense emotions and having an emotional breakdown lies in the duration of the experience and its impact on the individual. Intense emotions may be distressing and can somewhat disrupt a person's daily life but the individual still experiences a sense of relative control over their emotions and their life.

On the other hand, when someone is having an emotional breakdown, they may find it impossible to perform even the most basic tasks of daily life. This happens when a person's coping mechanisms become severely overwhelmed. It feels like life is completely spiraling out of control and the individual seems unable to control their own self.

It is important to note that learning to deal with intense emotions properly can help prevent the possibility of a complete breakdown. Events like the death of a loved one or severe loss of any kind are part of the human experience. Someone who hasn't developed the tools and trained their coping mechanisms to handle intense emotions can break down when an extreme event happens.

In this chapter, I want to empower you with the right kind of tools and techniques to manage intense emotions. By paying attention to your emotional world, you'll be able to live a more fulfilling life. Always remember that what doesn't get dealt with, gets stored somewhere else. Just because something is out of sight doesn't mean that it no longer impacts you. It is akin to stuffing all your clutter in one armoire. Your house may look clean on the surface but it is only a matter of time that the armoire will burst open and all the clutter will splatter all over your house once again.

I will also give you the tools and techniques for managing an emotional breakdown. You'll know what to do if you or someone else is having an emotional breakdown. As I said earlier, if you get in the habit of regularly dealing with your intense emotions as they arise, you'll minimize the possibility of having an emotional breakdown.

THE CALL-IT-OUT ALOUD TECHNIQUE

I call this technique call it out aloud because that's exactly what you do. When you are experiencing distressing emotions, don't try to suppress them or deny them. Instead, focus on accepting and acknowledging them. Accepting distressing emotions doesn't mean you have to act on them or mull on them. It simply means accepting that you are experiencing certain emotions at the moment and IT IS OKAY to allow yourself to have this experience.

You start talking to yourself saying exactly what is happening. Ideally, you want to be able to speak out aloud to yourself but if that's not possible, then you can also do the talking silently inside your mind. I would still strongly recommend that you find a space where you can be by yourself and then just speak out aloud to yourself. This really helps with the disassociation practice. When you are speaking inside your mind, it is easier to become lost in the maze of thoughts.

So what does this look in practice? Let us say you are experiencing anger. You will say to yourself, "I feel anger – extreme anger right now." Allow yourself to feel the anger in its full intensity. Again, it isn't something to be discarded, denied or suppressed. Sit with it – let it communicate with you.

Continue identifying, labeling, and acknowledging whatever is happening. For instance, your narration can be something like, "I feel very upset right now. My palms are sweating, my breathing is erratic, my heart is palpitating. I am feeling a fight-or-flight reaction in its full intensity. I honestly feel a massive urge to punch my boss. I feel the urge to shout, "How dare you talk to me like that?"

You acknowledge all the negative and "bad" things you are feeling the urge to do. This doesn't mean you have to act on them. You are simply acknowledging and accepting that a part of you has been so severely affected by the situation that you are feeling the urge to do something drastic. Something really magical begins to happen when you start accepting all your feelings, emotions, and urges as they are. After a while, you lose the urge to act on those destructive thoughts that arise in a moment of heightened emotions.

Intense emotions fog our ability to think clearly. We may feel tempted to do something that we will likely regret later. It is crucial to put off taking important decisions until you are feeling more balanced. In fact, never take any important decision when you are in a heightened emotional state – be it positive or negative emotions. Both extreme joy and extreme dejection can obfuscate your ability to think clearly. Important decisions should only be taken in a state of emotional equilibrium when you are neither too overwhelmed by positive emotions nor too dragged down by negative emotions.

VENTING THROUGH WRITING

Writing is a very powerful medium for processing and venting difficult emotions. I am often amazed by how relieved I feel every time I write down what I am feeling. In a heightened emotional state, I feel the urge to do something that I know I will regret later but once I write down everything I am feeling, the urge also passes away. Many times I have written down my feelings, emotions, and thoughts and by the end I felt like a different person.

The process is very simple. You just take a pen and a paper and start writing everything that is on your thinking and feeling. Don't censor yourself – don't try to be perfect with your writing. The writing is only for you. You don't have to worry about grammar or spelling. Just express yourself on paper. Yes, I would recommend that you do this exercise on paper. According to a study conducted by University of Tokyo, it was found that writing on paper engages the brain more powerfully than what can be achieved by writing on digital devices (University of Tokyo, 2021).

Writing with digital tools just doesn't feel the same. It can help process your thoughts but I always feel a more powerful sense of release and relief when I pour my difficult thoughts and emotions on paper. I would also recommend ritually letting them go by burning or tearing the paper and releasing the ashes or pieces in a flowing water body. If you don't have access to a flowing water body, then you can simply flush the paper. Just be careful if you are flushing pieces of paper instead of just the ashes. It might clog your toilet. Alternatively, you can bury the ashes or pieces in earth. Do whatever helps you feel better!

DEEP BREATHING

When you are in a heightened emotional state, your breathing automatically becomes erratic. The body and mind are strongly connected. Hence, one of the ways to get yourself to calm down is by focusing on the body. By breathing deeply, you'll start feeling more centered and grounded.

When you are overwhelmed, just shift your focus from what is troubling you onto your breathing. I know it is going to be tough to let go of it but tell yourself it is just for a few moments. You can go back to it after a while. This will trick the mind into loosening the grip on to distressing thoughts and emotions. Also, keep in mind that by constantly focusing on your troublesome thoughts and emotions, you can't solve a challenging situation. Solutions require feeling centered and calm.

For a few moments, just sit down with yourself. Close your eyes and breathe deeply. You can count from 1-8 for each inhalation and exhalation. So inhale 1-2-3-4-5-6-7-8. Exhale 1-2-3-4-5-6-7-8. To engage your body and mind further, you can also do the counting with your fingers while focusing on your breath.

If you can't close your eyes, then do the exercise with your eyes open but do it, please! Although I would strongly recommend doing it with your eyes closed. It really helps disconnect from the chaos you may be experiencing in your external reality.

You can also do this breathing technique when you are about to burst out or lash out on someone. When you are feeling the urge to act on that instinct, buy yourself a few moments. Just practice this breathing technique by focusing entirely on your breathing. You aren't saying you won't do what you are feeling the urge to do. You are just buying yourself a few moments after which you will be free to do whatever you must do.

After doing the breathing exercises you will be amazed to realize that the urge to take drastic action would have passed away. If it doesn't, just buy yourself a few more moments and continue doing this exercise. Also, do the other practices I am sharing in this chapter. Eventually, the urge to take drastic action will surely pass away and you will be glad it did!

MOVE YOUR BODY

As I said earlier, the body and mind are strongly connected. Just as the body can be influenced with the mind, the mind can also be influenced by the body. Intense emotions often cause muscle stiffness and a sense of stagnancy in the body and mind. One powerful solution for overcoming this state is by simply moving the body. I would highly recommend taking walks in nature. The refreshing and replenishing air in nature really helps with feeling centered and grounded – doesn't matter whether you are taking a walk in a public park or a seashore.

That being said, any kind of proper movement is good for the body. The human body isn't designed to be confined to a desk and chair for extended periods of time. The body thrives on movement. It is also a well-known fact that exercise produces endorphins or feel-good hormones. Physical movement is directly linked with a significant reduction in stress (Mayo Clinic Staff, 2022).

Whatever your choice of movement is, just get your body moving. Don't sit around and continue dwelling on what's vexing you. Do some yoga, tai chi, stretching, gym workouts, or simply take a walk.

POSITIVE SELF-TALK

We are all constantly conversing with ourselves in the silent alleys of our minds. Unfortunately, in most cases, this self-talk is extremely negative. It tends to be a never-ending barrage of criticism and constantly disparaging yourself. You may think it is your own inner voice saying all this to you. Hence, you accept it as the truth.

Your inner critic isn't really you. It is an internalized voice of your primary caregiver. When you were a small child, you were constantly told who you are, what you are capable of, what you aren't capable of. You didn't have enough experience or perspective on life to form your own opinions. You simply accepted what was told to you. Of course, some of it will be good that supports you in living a healthy and fulfilling life. Unfortunately, in most cases, the inner critic is all too loud. It constantly tells you what you cannot do or criticizes you so harshly that you feel debilitated by it.

I am not suggesting that you should blame your primary caregivers. In most cases, parents want the best for their children. However, people are not perfect. Human beings have a tendency of projecting on to others what they believe to be true for themselves. If they believe they can't do something, they'll tell you that you can't do it either. We also can't ignore the fact that we live in a highly chaotic world. Very few people are truly in touch with themselves or have their intellectual and emotional lives together. Parents unwittingly pass on their unhealed trauma and dysfunctional behavior patterns onto their children.

The good news is that most of the negative behavioral and thought patterns we suffer from are things we have learned from others. If we can learn something negative unwittingly, then we can also unlearn it. With intention, purpose, knowledge, and determination, we can retrain ourselves to be the type of person we truly want to be. You have the power to live life on your own terms and be the highest version of yourself!

The first step you must take is to become aware of your self-talk. Throughout the day, pause for a few minutes every couple of hours, and ask yourself, "What am I thinking and feeling right now?" Observe what your mind is telling you. You can also use the narration technique I shared with you earlier to state to yourself what is going on with you.

Once you start spotting the negative self-talk, ask yourself, "Is this really true? What evidence do I have that this is true? What evidence I have that this is not true?" Once you start compelling yourself to think logically, you'll realize that most of the self-criticism is largely illogical. There is no basis for why you should believe those negative things about yourself.

However, the inner critic has been programmed over years. It isn't going to be defeated that easily. You must replace criticisms with positive self-talk. Let us assume this is what your inner critic is saying, "I am so bad at this. I just can't do anything right." You can replace this with, "I have the power and the ability to be good at anything I truly commit to. I know I can do anything I set my mind upon!" Say it out aloud to reinforce the idea further. If that's not possible, then simply keep repeating the new positive affirmation inside your mind.

You want to talk to yourself like your best friend. What will you say to your best friend if they were struggling with self-doubt or were constantly criticizing themselves? You also want to become your own greatest cheerleader. If you start feeling exhausted or self-doubt begins creeping in, encourage yourself like a cheerleader, "Come on, you can do this!" "You've got this. Keep going!" "I know I can do this!"

This kind of positive cheerleading will provide you the energy to keep pushing and preserving to achieve your goals.

HOW TO DEAL WITH AN EMOTIONAL BREAKDOWN

Having an emotional breakdown in the face of an extreme event is not something out of the ordinary. It is possible to overcome such a breakdown on your own, especially with the help of loving family members and friends. But if the breakdown persists for an extremely long duration to the extent that it cripples one's work and social life, it may become necessary to seek professional help.

In this section, I will highlight what you can do if you or someone you know is having an emotional breakdown. All the techniques I shared in the previous section are also useful for dealing with an emotional breakdown but here are some additional things that one should focus on when undergoing such a difficult experience.

FOCUS ON MAINTAINING A ROUTINE

I know how hard this is but you must make the effort to create a routine for yourself. Your daily routine is the first thing that goes out of the window when a breakdown occurs but one of the most effective techniques for bringing a sense of balance to your life is also by going back to that routine. Of course, it is going to be extremely challenging but simply doing what you need to do helps you move your body and that's what initiates the healing process.

Try to go to bed at a set time and wake up at a set time. I know this is easier said than done but you must make the effort. If you don't know how you are going to get through life, shift your focus to something smaller by asking yourself, "What's the one thing I need to do right now" and just do it. It can be something as simple as washing your plate and putting it back where it belongs or folding your clothes and putting them away.

Don't see your daily routine as a burden but as a means for finding comfort. You will find a sense of familiarity and a degree of harmony in maintaining your daily routine.

INVEST IN SELF-CARE

Be extremely gentle and compassionate with yourself – you deserve it. Take the time to look after yourself. Pamper yourself as much as you can. Cook your favorite meals if you can or allow yourself to order your favorite food. Never feel guilty about looking after yourself. You are worth the effort, time, money, and resources!

SPEND TIME WITH TRUSTED LOVED ONES

Try to spend time with others who love and support you. When you are with them don't just talk about all your distressing emotions and thoughts. Instead, focus on doing something fun together. For instance, you can go to an amusement park together or do something else that both parties enjoy. Spending time with loved ones is extremely therapeutic and healing.

JOIN SUPPORT GROUPS

More often than not, the only people who can truly understand what we are going through are other people who are either still undergoing a similar experience or who have been through it in the past. Finding a local or online support group for your specific issue can be an excellent resource for overcoming an emotional breakdown.

You can ask for assistance from people who have overcome similar challenges – learn what they did and try their methods and techniques for yourself. Try to learn as much as possible about how other people are coping with their challenges – what works for them and what doesn't. Support groups can really be an exceptional resource for finding practical solutions and techniques for overcoming one's challenges. You also find understanding and compassion with others who have been through or are going through something similar. That can truly be a huge blessing!

8

PRACTICING MINDFULNESS, MEDITATION, AND GUIDED JOURNALING EXERCISES

"The issues we often run away from and refuse to address, are the very things that end up transforming our lives when we choose and commit to healing from buried emotional wounds."

— KEMI SOGUNLE

In this chapter, I want to share with you some more practical tools that you can use in your daily life to overcome toxic thinking and dysfunctional behavior patterns. You can use these tools whenever you are feeling stressed and/or overwhelmed. You can also use them every day as daily practices to support yourself in living a healthy life.

The more often you do these practices, the greater will be the benefits you derive from them. But even if you do them only once in a while, they will help you calm down and regain focus.

The important thing to always remember is that difficult and painful emotions should never be suppressed. They should be faced, embraced, and dealt with. I have said this before and I will say it again. All your emotions are there to support you in living a full and meaningful life. Never fall for the temptation of shutting some away and embracing only a few. What gets suppressed continues to impact our life in ways we do not even recognize.

Most people live a life of incessant distraction. Thanks to the abundance of technology, it is easier now than ever to find a new distraction to constantly keep oneself preoccupied. I observe how people turn off the computer only to switch on the TV. When they finally turn off the TV, they pick up their phones whiling away endless hours meaninglessly browsing the internet. The internet is a wonderful place to learn new skills, acquire new knowledge, and connect with other interesting people. But undisciplined use of the internet can also be very damaging. The key word here is to be intentional with your time.

Whatever you are doing, do it with mindfulness. Don't watch TV or play video games only to distract yourself. In fact, distraction at its core is an instinct to avoid pain. For instance, you sit down to write a business report. The task is painful and requires you to concentrate. To avoid the pain, you seek distractions like checking your email or browsing social media.

I am not suggesting that you should give up TV, social media, or anything else. I am just advocating for using the tools available at your disposal with intention and purpose to create the kind of life YOU want to live. There is a difference between using these tools for your own benefit and allowing them to dominate your life because you didn't clarify how you should be utilizing them in the first place.

The same can be said for food. Don't eat when you are bored, tired, or in emotional pain. Eat to nourish your body. Feed yourself high-quality nutritious food that will support you in living a healthy life. Emotional eating is a huge problem in modern-day society. Most people eat way more than what their body actually needs and worse than that, they are eating food devoid of any real nutrition.

Research suggests that a wholesome Mediterranean diet can really help with emotional regulation (Holt, Lee, Morton, Tonstad, 2014). The Mediterranean diet focuses heavily on the consumption of whole grains, fruits, vegetables, nuts, beans, fish, and some meat. I would encourage you to focus on eating fresh wholesome food. Stay away from packaged meals that contain a lot of chemicals and additives. Living a healthy life requires thinking healthily.

Once you start focusing on making healthier choices, you will eat differently and make different choices. Try to move your body as much as possible. Instead of taking the elevator, take the stairs. Instead of munching on fries, opt for the apple. Initially, it may be difficult to make these healthy choices but over time, you will train your taste buds to start liking wholesome food items more.

PRACTICING MINDFULNESS

Most of our pain and suffering is often not in the present but in the memory of the past or in anticipation of the future. Mindfulness is a powerful practice because it allows you to fully inhabit the present moment. Instead of allowing your mind to wander here and there, you bring it to be fully present with your body in the here and now.

Most of our problems and suffering disappear when our consciousness fully inhabits the present moment. I really believe that heaven and hell reside within the mind. Untamed thoughts and emotions can give you the experience of living in hell. On the other hand, a calm and stable mind can give you the experience of heaven on earth.

Research also shows that mindfulness practices are extremely beneficial for managing emotional dysregulation (Guendelman, Medeiros, Rampes, 2017). In this section, I want to share with you a simple mindfulness practice that you can do any time of the day. You don't need to be in a specific type of place to do it nor do you need special props and tools. Mindfulness is the act of becoming fully present in the moment with whatever you are doing. It also increases your focus. Hence, it boosts your performance as well.

You can do this mindfulness exercise lying down or while sitting in a chair. You can also do it while taking a walk in nature or while doing gentle stretches. You can close your eyes if you are lying down or sitting in a chair. If you are taking a walk, then obviously you'll have to keep your eyes open. There are no rules except to just become present with yourself and inhabit the present moment fully.

THE PRACTICE

Find a place where you can be by yourself for this practice. Sit up straight if you are sitting up in a chair. If you are lying down or walking, then make sure that your back is straight. Before beginning the practice, it is important to get your body in proper posture. If possible, close your eyes.

Focus on your breath – notice how each breath is going in and observe how each breath comes out. Focus all your attention on the in-flow and out-flow of breath. Focus on your breathing as if the entire world has dissolved for now. All that exists in this moment is your breath – the in-flow and out-flow of breath is all there is for now.

With each inhalation, observe how the breath is entering through your nose gently touching your nostrils and then spreading through your entire body. As the breath spreads through your body, it is rejuvenating and replenishing each body part. Your body, mind, and soul are being transformed by the power of this breath. You are becoming the highest and finest version of yourself through the power of each inhalation.

As you exhale, feel all the accumulated tension, stress, pain, and suffering melting away. With each exhalation, release all that is unwanted. As the breath moves out of your body and exits through your nose, it is taking away with you every-thing that no longer serves you. You are feeling light, restful, and joyful as you have been freed from everything that was previously weighing you down.

Continue taking deep breaths, visualizing how each breath is filling you with hope, positivity, joy, and happiness. With each exhalation, continue releasing everything that no longer serves you. You can also visualize each in-breath as a fresh green-colored energy that enters your body to replenish and rejuvenate your body, mind, and soul. You can visualize each out breath as a dark brown-colored energy that you are expelling out of your system.

Continue breathing deeply – with each inhalation your chest and stomach expand. With each exhalation, your chest and stomach are contracting. Focus on this deep breathing. Your body and mind are becoming relaxed. If thoughts arise, witness them. Don't dismiss any thought. Don't cling on to any thought. Your mind is like an infinite ocean. Each thought is like a wave that arises and subsides of its own accord. You are sitting on the seashore simply watching the waves arise and subside.

Continue focusing on your breath but now also become aware of your surroundings. What are the sounds you can hear now? What are you smelling? What kind of taste do you have in your mouth right now? If your eyes are open, then observe what your eyes are seeing. Become fully present in the here and now. Observe the world around you without judging it. Just be present with it. Observe the world as if it were a movie playing out in front of your eyes. Just watch, feel, and experience it. Do not resist or reject anything.

For as long as you feel comfortable, you can continue doing this exercise. Remain focused on your breath and just observe both your inner and outer world. If any judgment or thought arises, witness it like a wave arising and subsiding in the vast ocean of your consciousness.

When you are ready, take a few more deep breaths to ground yourself. Rub your palms together, place them on your closed eyelids and gently open your eyes. If your eyes were open, then just move your body slightly vigorously.

MINDFULNESS ON THE GO

Practicing mindfulness as you go about your day is very powerful for remaining focused and doing your best at every task you undertake. Practicing mindfulness on the go is deceptively simple. I am saying "deceptively simple" because it seems very simple on the surface but that doesn't mean it is easy to practice. It does require a considerable amount of effort at least at the beginning. However, I would say it is totally worth the effort.

So what does mindfulness on the go look like? You can practice it anytime and anywhere. Just ask yourself "What am I doing right now?" "Where is my mind right now?" "Is my mind fully present with my body right now?" If you find your mind wandering, then gently bring it into the present moment to fully inhabit your body. Allow yourself to feel your body. For instance, if you are typing on your keyboard, then feel the sensation of your finger touching the keyboard fully.

If you are walking, allow yourself to feel what the ground beneath your feet feels like while you are walking. Being fully present inside your body means experiencing the present moment with all your five senses. The easiest way to get yourself to fully inhabit your body and the present moment is by focusing on what your five senses are communicating to you. What are you seeing? What are you smelling? What are you hearing? What are you tasting? What are you touching?

You can practice this while doing any task. It will compel you to be fully present with and focus on whatever you are doing. This is the key to productivity!

STRESS RELEASE MEDITATION

Mental and emotional stress can make you very dysregulated. To practice emotional regulation, it is very important that you release stress from the body and mind on a regular basis. You can record this meditation in your own voice and listen to it every day or whenever you are feeling particularly stressed out.

I would highly recommend that you maintain a dedicated corner in your house for practicing meditation. This way, in your mind, that space will become associated with stress release and relaxation. Every time you sit down or lie down there, your mind will signal to your body it is time to relax. Yes, you can do this exercise in bed as well but I would recommend having a separate corner in your house set aside for meditation. The goal is also to remain in a state of relaxed wakefulness throughout the meditation and not to fall asleep. Since your bed is associated with sleeping, it is highly likely that you will fall asleep while doing the meditation practice.

That being said, if you have trouble sleeping, then you can certainly use this meditation as a tool to manage your insomnia. In that case, you can definitely do it in bed lying down. I would still recommend that you additionally practice it solely as a meditation practice for deep relaxation at another time of the day as well. This will help you train your body to remain in a state of relaxed wakefulness throughout the day and over time, you'll build the skill to evoke such a state at will.

THE PRACTICE

Find a quiet space where no one will disturb you. Sit down comfortably and close your eyes.

Focus your mind on your breathing. Breathe deeply. With each inhalation, your chest and stomach expand. With each exhalation, your chest and stomach contract. To keep your mind focused you can count to 8 for each inhalation and exhalation. Inhale 1-2-3-4-5-6-7-8. Exhale 1-2-3-4-5-6-7-8. Continue breathing deeply. With each inhalation, feel yourself getting renewed and refreshed. With each exhalation, release all the tension and accumulated stress from your body and mind.

Now that you are feeling grounded and centered, take your focus to your toes. Feel your toes. If there is tension, release it with the next exhalation. As you inhale, say to yourself, "I am relaxing my toes. My toes are completely relaxed." As you exhale, release all stress and tension from your toes.

Focus on the soles of your feet and release any tension you are feeling right now. As you inhale, say to yourself, "I am relaxing the soles of my feet. The soles of my feet are completely relaxed." As you exhale, release all stress and tension from the soles of your feet.

Focus on the top of your feet and release any tension you are feeling right now. As you inhale, say to yourself, "I am relaxing the top of my feet. The top of my feet are completely relaxed." As you exhale, release all stress and tension from the top of your feet.

Focus on your ankles and bottom legs. As you inhale, say to yourself, "I am relaxing my ankles and bottom legs. My ankles and bottom legs are completely relaxed." As you exhale, release all stress and tension from your ankles and bottom legs.

Focus on your upper legs. As you inhale, say to yourself, "I am relaxing my upper legs. My upper legs are completely relaxed." As you exhale, release all stress and tension from your upper legs.

Focus on your hips. As you inhale, say to yourself, "I am relaxing my hips. My hips are completely relaxed." As you exhale, release all stress and tension from your hips.

Focus on your stomach and lower back. As you inhale, say to yourself, "I am relaxing my stomach and lower back. My stomach and lower back are completely relaxed." As you exhale, release all stress and tension from your stomach and lower back.

Focus on your chest and upper back. As you inhale, say to yourself, "I am relaxing my chest and upper back. My chest and upper back are completely relaxed." As you exhale, release all stress and tension from your chest and upper back.

Focus on your wrist and palms. As you inhale, say to yourself, "I am relaxing my wrist and palms. My wrist and palms are completely relaxed." As you exhale, release all stress and tension from your wrist and palms.

Focus on your elbows and lower arms. As you inhale, say to yourself, "I am relaxing my elbows and lower arms. My elbows and lower arms are completely relaxed." As you exhale, release all stress and tension from your elbows and lower arms.

Focus on your upper arms. As you inhale, say to yourself, "I am relaxing my upper arms. My upper arms are completely relaxed." As you exhale, release all stress and tension from your upper arms.

Focus on your shoulders and neck. As you inhale, say to yourself, "I am relaxing my shoulders and neck. My shoulders and neck are completely relaxed." As you exhale, release all stress and tension from your shoulders and neck.

Focus on your eyes and face. As you inhale, say to yourself, "I am relaxing my eyes and face. My eyes and face are completely relaxed." As you exhale, release all stress and tension from your eyes and face.

Focus on your head and skull. As you inhale, say to yourself, "I am relaxing my head and skull. My head and skull are completely relaxed." As you exhale, release all stress and tension from your head and skull.

You are now deeply relaxed. Every part of your body is deeply relaxed. Your mind is also deeply relaxed. Allow yourself to fully savor this state of deep relaxation. Just breathe deeply. With each inhalation, your chest and stomach are expanding. With each exhalation, your chest and stomach are contracting. Continue breathing deeply. Feel yourself fully inhabiting your body.

When you are ready, slowly move your fingers and toes. Rub your palms together and gently place them on your eyelids. Slowly open your eyes while still retaining that sense of deep restfulness in your body and mind.

GUIDED JOURNALING EXERCISES

The goal of these exercises is to help you develop self-awareness. As I have said many times, emotional regulation requires intense self-awareness. You must regularly get in touch with yourself to fully appreciate and experience your emotional life. All emotions are to be felt, acknowledged, and embraced. You don't have to become fixated on them or mull over them but be willing to hear what they are trying to communicate with you.

You can copy these questions in another journal and use them regularly to get in touch with yourself. You can pick just a few of these questions to answer regularly or you can use all of them. You can do the exercises every day or once in a while. It is all up to you and what works best for you.

THE PRACTICE

What is the predominant emotion you are feeling right now?

_____

_____

_____

_____

Where in your body do you feel this emotion most intensely?

_____

_____

_____

What is the message that this emotion is trying to convey to you? What can you learn about your life from the experience of this emotion? Is it telling you that you are moving in the right direction or is it signaling you to make some changes?

_____

_____

_____

If you feel you must make some changes to your life, then list down exactly what those changes should be.

Is there any emotion you are avoiding right now?

Why are you avoiding this emotion?

Give yourself just five minutes to fully feel this emotion that you are avoiding. You can time an alarm clock for five minutes if you wish. Tell yourself that you have to feel this emotion only for five minutes, after that you can go back to avoiding it if you wish. Now, feel this emotion fully – really try listening to this emotion. What is this emotion trying to convey to you and why is it so painful for you to hear what it has to tell you?

_____

_____

_____

_____

If you feel you must make some changes to your life based on what this emotion is conveying to you, then list down exactly what those changes should be.

_____

_____

_____

_____

A SHORT MESSAGE FROM THE AUTHOR

Hey, are you enjoying the book? I'd love to hear your thoughts!

Many readers do not know how hard reviews are to come by, and how much they help an author.

I would be incredibly grateful if you could take just 60 seconds to write a brief review on Amazon, even if it's just a few sentences!

Thank you for taking the time to share your thoughts!

Your review will genuinely make a difference for me and help gain exposure for my work.

S. S. Leigh

CONCLUSION

I want to thank you for placing your trust in me and taking this journey together. I really hope this book has added tremendous value to your life. I would urge you to not treat it as a one-time read but keep coming back to it regularly. Emotional regulation is a skill that is built over time with consistent practice. Reading a book provides you with knowledge but skill is built only with practice. The more frequently you use the tools, techniques, methods, and ideas I have shared in this book, the more resilient you'll become.

May this be a new beginning for you! Always keep in mind that the quality of your inner world determines and influences the quality of your outer reality. You cannot change anything outside without first working on your inner world. We create the circumstances of our life based on the type of person we have been so far along the way. To live a different kind of life, we have to transform ourselves into the type of person who is truly capable of living our ideal lifestyle.

Life is about learning and growing. The more you learn, the more skills you build – the more you grow. With perpetual growth, you are guaranteed to keep upgrading and leveling up your life. Who you want to be and how you want to live your life is in your own hands. No matter what kind of cards you have been dealt with, you can get the best out of yourself and out of life. It is all about adopting and practicing the right attitude.

When life strikes you down, don't allow yourself to writhe in self-pity. Allow yourself to feel the pain and shed a few tears, then focus all your energy on getting back up. No matter what happens, you can always come back stronger and better. The wheels of destiny are compelled to favor those who constantly seek more and refuse to settle for anything less than what they truly desire. While you are going after your dreams, be sure to keep yourself centered and grounded by practicing the emotional regulation techniques, tools, and methods you have learned. Love yourself and take care of yourself. You are worthy of it!

Self-love and self-care should be a way of life for all of us. We can create a beautiful life for ourselves and for our loved ones, only when we truly love ourselves. If you are looking for more practical tools and techniques, then you may want to check out my *I am Capable of Anything* series which has unique daily affirmations for each day of the year. If self-love is an area of real struggle for you, then you may also want to check out my *Radical Self-Love* book.

Sincerely,

S.S. Leigh

REFERENCES

Attachment Theory. Wikipedia. (n.d.). Retrieved January 28, 2023, from https://en.wikipedia.org/wiki/Attachment_theory

Bergland, C. (2015, May 9). *How Do Your Genes Influence Levels of Emotional Sensitivity?* Psychology Today. Retrieved January 28, 2023, from https://www.psychologytoday.com/us/blog/the-athletes-way/201505/how-do-your-genes-influence-levels-emotional-sensitivity

Card, O. S. (n.d.). **Quoted in** Goodreads. Retrieved January 28, 2023, from https://www.goodreads.com/quotes/19828-this-is-how-humans-are-we-question-all-our-beliefs

Chopra, D. (n.d.). **Quoted in** BrainyQuote. Retrieved January 28, 2023, from https://www.brainyquote.com/quotes/deepak_chopra_453950

Cloud, H. (n.d.). *Quoted in* Goodreads. Retrieved January 28, 2023, from https://www.goodreads.com/quotes/790608-boundaries-define-us-they-define-what-is-me-and-what

DeLoach, N. (n.d.). *Quoted in* AZ Quotes. Retrieved January 28, 2023, from https://www.azquotes.com/quote/1511617

Dweck, C. S. (2007). *Mindset: The New Psychology of Success.* Ballantine Books.

Guendelman, S., Medeiros, S., & Rampes, H. (2017, March 6). *Mindfulness and emotion regulation: Insights from neurobiological, psychological, and clinical studies.* Frontiers. Retrieved January 28, 2023, from https://www.frontiersin.org/articles/10.3389/fpsyg.2017.00220/full

Holt, M. E., Lee, J. W., Morton, K. R., & Tonstad, S. (2014). *Mediterranean diet and Emotion Regulation.* NCBI. Retrieved January 28, 2023, from https://www.ncbi.nlm.nih.gov/pmc/articles/PMC6350904/

Kiyosaki, R. T. (n.d.). *Quoted in* Goodreads. Retrieved January 28, 2023, from https://www.goodreads.com/quotes/1185231-learn-to-use-your-emotions-to-think-not-think-with

Mayer, J. D. (n.d.). *Quoted in* Quotefancy. Retrieved January 28, 2023, from https://quotefancy.com/quote/1714976

Mayo Clinic Staff. (2022, August 3). *Exercise and stress: Get moving to manage stress.* Mayo Clinic. Retrieved January 28, 2023, from https://www.mayoclinic.org/healthy-lifestyle/stress-managment/in-depth/exercise-and-stress/art-20044469

McEwen, B. S. (2003, August). *Early Life Influences on Life-Long Patterns of Behavior and Health*. PubMed. Retrieved January 28, 2023, from https://pubmed.ncbi.nlm.nih.gov/12953293/

Nagda, H. (n.d.). *Quoted in* Goodreads. Retrieved January 28, 2023, from https://www.goodreads.com/author/quotes/21178772

Nicolai, E. (n.d.). *Quoted in* Goodreads. Retrieved January 28, 2023, from https://www.goodreads.com/author/quotes/7303179.ELLE_NICOLAI

Robbins, M. (2017). *The 5 Second Rule: Transform Your Life, Work, and Confidence with Everyday Courage*. Mel Robbins Productions Inc.

Rohn, J. (n.d.). *Quoted in* Goodreads. Retrieved January 28, 2023, from https://www.goodreads.com/quotes/1798-you-are-the-average-of-the-five-people-you-spend

Socrates. (n.d.). *Quoted in* BrainyQuote. Retrieved January 28, 2023, from https://www.brainyquote.com/quotes/socrates_101168

Sogunle, K. (n.d.). *Quoted in* Goodreads. Retrieved January 28, 2023, from https://www.goodreads.com/work/quotes/53979331-beyond-the-pain-by-kemi-sogunle

Stone, W. C. (n.d.). *Quoted in* BrainyQuote. Retrieved January 28, 2023, from https://www.brainyquote.com/quotes/w_clement_stone_193778

Tahir, S. (n.d.). *Quoted in* Goodreads. Retrieved January 28, 2023, from https://www.goodreads.com/quotes/7778144-your-emotions-make-you-human-even-the-unpleasant-ones-have

Thought. Wikipedia. (n.d.). Retrieved January 28, 2023, from https://en.wikipedia.org/wiki/Thought

University of Tokyo. (2021, March 19). *Study shows stronger brain activity after writing on paper than on tablet or smartphone.* ScienceDaily. Retrieved January 28, 2023, from https://www.sciencedaily.com/releases/2021/03/210319080820.htm

What is Behavior? NSW Health. (n.d.). Retrieved January 28, 2023, from https://www.health.nsw.gov.au/mental-health/psychosocial/principles/Pages/behaviour-whatis.aspx

Williams, A. (n.d.). *Quoted in* 60 *Law of Attraction Quotes to Boost Your Willpower.* Quote Ambition. Retrieved January 28, 2023, from https://www.quoteambition.com/law-of-attraction-quotes/

Made in the USA
Monee, IL
21 August 2023

41413312R00105